WILLIE CARSON

THE ILLUSTRATED BIOGRAPHY

MICHAEL SEELY was born in 1926; his father, Jim Seely, trained and rode his own horses and twice completed the Grand National course. Michael inherited the family love of racing, and joined *Raceform*, the official form-book, in 1965; he was appointed Northern Correspondent of *The Times* in 1975, and later became Racing Correspondent. He has also been a regular contributor to *The Field* and *Pacemaker*; he was given the Clive Graham Award for Racing Journalist of the Year, jointly in 1980 and outright in 1989. Michael Seely lives in Nottinghamshire; this is his first book.

WILLIE CARSON

THE ILLUSTRATED BIOGRAPHY

MICHAEL SEELY

HEADLINE

OVERLEAF *Muddied but unbowed.*
Carson, with trademark grin, in 1974

Designed by Adrian Morris

Picture research by Ivor Game

Typeset by Avocet Typesetters, Bicester, Oxon

Illustration reproduction by
Brian Gregory Associates Ltd

Printed and bound in Great Britain by
Butler and Tanner Limited, Frome

HEADLINE BOOK PUBLISHING PLC
Headline House
79 Great Titchfield Street
London W1P 7FN

First published in 1991
by HEADLINE BOOK PUBLISHING PLC

First published in paperback in 1992
by HEADLINE BOOK PUBLISHING PLC

10 9 8 7 6 5 4 3 2 1

ISBN 0 7472 7921 7

CONTENTS

*Carson punches the air to salute Nashwan's win
in the 1989 2,000 Guineas at Newmarket*

INTRODUCTION

Willie Carson punched the air in triumph. He had always known Nashwan was a good horse, maybe even a great one, and now, returning to the winner's enclosure after the 1989 2,000 Guineas, everyone knew. Carson could be forgiven his unabashed display of euphoria. Since the golden years of the late seventies and early eighties, when he had ridden Classic winners with comforting regularity, his career had slid inexorably into the doldrums. No longer guaranteed quality mounts, his moods had darkened and his relationship with the press sailed close to venomous.

Then, when his fortunes could apparently sink no lower, Dick Hern, his retaining trainer, was crippled in a hunting accident and confined to a wheelchair. Carson had become deeply discontented. Without Nashwan, Carson would almost certainly have hung up his boots, and in doing so denied himself a remarkable Indian summer which was to return him to the heights of his profession. 'Every time I get on the horse it's like making love,' he was to say in a moment of awe. Yet Carson had gone into that season with an enviable choice of possible Classic mounts. Both Prince Of Dance and Al Hareb, trained, like Nashwan, by Hern, had high-class two-year-old form. Carson had his choice, and he was determined to be right.

But, suddenly, as Christmas gave way to the New Year, the Nashwan dream threatened to become a nightmare. The colt developed a splint, a horseman's term for a bony growth, on his near foreleg. He was lame. Although the setback was not serious for his long-term health, the only cure was complete rest.

Prince Of Dance and Al Hareb began serious work in February but Nashwan, although now restored to full fitness, was a month behind their preparations. However, Nashwan began to fizz. The setback was beginning to look less and less important as he became the equal of his stable companions at home.

'It suddenly started to dawn on everyone that although we'd been thinking of Nashwan as our Derby horse, he could be our best hope for the Guineas as well,' Neil Graham, Hern's assistant, says. 'He was working so well. Prince Of Dance was going all right but no more, and Al Hareb was showing none of his old sparkle. All of a sudden everything pointed towards Nashwan.' Carson was as aware of it as anyone. As Nashwan began working with ever greater verve, Carson's eagerness took over. Keen for even faster progress, Carson clashed with Hern over the handling of the colt. The trainer, anxious not to push Nashwan too hard before he was ready for more work, found Carson determined – too determined – to press ahead.

One morning, as Hern and Carson met for their usual post-gallop conference at the window of Hern's station wagon, the jockey urged more action. 'He wants faster work than that 'gov'nor,' he said. The criticism nettled Hern. 'He's all right, Willie,' Hern said curtly. 'That will do for now.'

Despite the favourable noises emanating from West Ilsley about Nashwan's progress, Carson had not given any indication of his Guineas mount. Bookmakers and punters wrestled daily with West Ilsley's version of the three-card trick. The question of Carson's ride in the Guineas was paramount; opinions shifted regularly as each of the three possibles enjoyed their day in the spotlight. But there were few solid clues forthcoming; Carson and Hern would not be hurried.

Then, one weekend in April, it all slotted together. I was staying near the Herns for the Newbury spring meeting and decided the time had come to find the answer. Simple in theory, formidable in practice. Not for nothing does Major Hern have a reputation for being tight-lipped. He positively revels in the cloak-and-dagger atmosphere of secrecy and so-called privileged information surrounding stable plans. A touch of the George Smiley technique would be required to prise open the oyster.

Friday evening found Hern ensconced in his wheelchair, savouring a glass of champagne before dinner. Fishing for information, I tossed what I believed would be a fairly innocuous observation to the Major. 'Punters are taking the 40–1 on offer about Nashwan for the Guineas,' I remarked. The gambit sat like an orphan in the silence as Hern weighed his response. Eventually he replied: 'If Nashwan were to run in the Guineas, 40–1 would be a good price.' This deceptively simple remark was like an alarm clanging. It amounted not only to an admission that Nashwan was in the same class as Prince Of Dance and Al Hareb, but that the 'dark horse' was delighting his trainer on the gallops. An early-morning visit to the gallops merely acted as confirmation. Even to my comparatively untutored eye Nashwan's ground-devouring stride screamed his well-being.

Some serious betting was called for. The following afternoon, the day of the Greenham Stakes at Newbury, I placed bets of £100 each on Nashwan for the 2,000 Guineas and Derby at 25–1 and 16–1 respectively, and a £50 each-way double at 100–1 for the two races. Unfortunately, some serious loss of nerve was also evident.

The next morning I telephoned Ladbrokes, with whom I had placed the bet, to halve the stakes. It was a decision I was to regret, and the reason was not long delayed. Sheikh Hamdan had been pressing Hern for a decision to run Nashwan in the Guineas, so the following Saturday Hern arranged a work for Nashwan with Misbah, a good-class handicapper acquired primarily as a lead horse for the high-class middle-distance performer Unfuwain.

Carson rode Nashwan, with Brian Procter, Hern's number one work rider, on

Chief work rider Brian Procter waits as Willie chats to Dick Hern on the training gallops at West Ilsley

Misbah. 'The work was over a mile,' said Procter. 'I led them for six furlongs and then Willie and Nashwan came past us as though we were standing still. With a furlong still to go they were pulling up, just a speck in the distance.' Even Hern was awestruck. 'In all my years at West Ilsley I've never seen a horse work like that,' he said.

The work was the cue for a Keystone Kops like rush to telephone the bookmakers. Lads sprinted to their cars and bicycles or just dashed headlong for the nearest phone. This was the investment of a lifetime and no one wanted to miss out. Everyone in the stable, from the highest to the lowest, had backed Nashwan.

As Graham returned to the yard, having supervised the start of the gallop, the atmosphere crackled. 'I remember the Major being his usual conservative self, just saying things like "He worked extremely well". Willie was exactly the opposite. He was so excited he couldn't sit down to breakfast. It was all he could do to keep from jumping around the room. His eyes were popping out of his head.'

With Al Hareb still under a cloud after a defeat in the Craven Stakes at Newmarket and Prince Of Dance looking increasingly likely to tackle longer distances than the Guineas mile, Carson's mount in the Guineas was resolved. The two weeks between the gallop and the 2,000 Guineas were vintage Carson. All reticence and caution were thrown to the winds; here was a man who knew he was holding the ace in the pack and was hell-bent on playing his hand to the maximum. The change was hammered home to me during a telephone conversation after a pre-Classic work by Nashwan. 'Have you backed him for the Guineas?' he screamed down the line.

'Yes,' I replied, 'at 25–1.'

'Don't hedge a penny of it,' he said, the voice becoming even more urgent. 'Back him again now at 8–1 and when he goes down to 4–1 have some more. Nashwan will win the Guineas.'

All this, just a fortnight before the big race, from a man who could make Tony Hancock look like an incurable optimist. Rival jockeys and trainers were given the full Carson treatment as he demanded to know how they could even think about taking on Nashwan at Newmarket; how they might as well stay at home, avoid Nashwan and save themselves the humiliation of crushing defeat. When Carson cranked up the propaganda machine there were no half measures. The vastly experienced trainers Michael Stoute and Guy Harwood, the trainers of the strongly fancied Guineas candidates Shaadi and Exbourne, admitted to being impressed by the hype.

Carson's confidence was boundless. Stoute's stable jockey, Walter Swinburn, was buttonholed by Carson and informed: 'I don't know why you're bothering to run Shaadi. Stoute is wasting his time.' Even Steve Cauthen, no stranger to big-race pressures and a graduate of the much fiercer American school of race riding, was sufficiently shaken to take Procter to one side at Brighton races and ask: 'Is Nashwan really as good as that?'

He was soon to have his answer. Carson flew to the three-day Guineas meeting, his belief in Nashwan undiminished. Hern and his wife Sheilah established themselves at their base in Lowther Street. Carson drew a blank on the opening day but the Friday produced two important wins with the successes of Prince Of Dance and Unfuwain. Although neither was a direct pointer to the chances of Nashwan, everyone associated with a Classic runner likes to see evidence of a stable in form. Punters took the hint and piled money on Nashwan, driving his price down from 4–1 to 3–1, the first time he had been favourite for the race.

Saturday dawned, and with it the moment of truth. In the quiet before the race, Hern and Carson reflected on what Nashwan meant to the stable. Their fortunes, just a few years before at such a low ebb, were reviving steadily. Yet for both of them Nashwan had become a talisman, the chance to return them to the very highest levels of racing. Neither now were young men; if Nashwan failed to live up to expectations, who could tell when the next great opportunity would come along? Would it come at all?

The race had a further significance. The Queen and Lord Carnarvon had refused to extend Hern's lease at West Ilsley when it expired at the end of 1989, a decision widely condemned by the press and public. Hern was seen as a loyal man who had been shabbily treated. Now, through Nashwan, he could present the best possible advertisement for his skills; that, despite his infirmity, he could still train top-class racehorses, and train them as well as anybody in the game.

In a field of fourteen, Nashwan started the 3–1 favourite. The principal dangers looked to be Shaadi, Exbourne, Danehill and Saratogan, trained in Ireland by the legendary Vincent O'Brien. Shaadi had beaten Exbourne in the Craven Stakes, a recognised Guineas trial, at Newmarket to underline his claim, but Pat Eddery, given the choice of Exbourne and Danehill, had opted for Danehill, the winner of the European Free Handicap, also at Newmarket.

In the parade ring Nashwan looked trained to the minute, all muscled authority as he circled the paddock. Carson mounted and sat quietly in the saddle. He leaned forward, patted Nashwan's neck, his eyes alert but preoccupied. They were led out on to the track, Carson and Nashwan oblivious to the crowds and their cries of encouragement. They had come here to do a job. Tactics would be vital. Nashwan's pedigree suggested stamina would be his forte; his rivals had speed to burn. That dictated that Carson would have to force the pace to draw the finishing speed from the opposition. Curiously, Nashwan was helped by Harwood's decision to run a

pacemaker, Greensmith, to ensure a strong gallop for Exbourne. There was at least an equal chance that it would be Nashwan, not Exbourne, who would reap the rewards of Greensmith's presence.

When the field came into view on the demanding straight Rowley Mile, Greensmith led with three furlongs to run. But he was beginning to falter as Carson had Nashwan poised to challenge up the middle of the track. As Greensmith dropped away, Carson seized the initiative. Two and a half furlongs out he asked Nashwan for a decisive effort, and the response was immediate. Nashwan burst into the lead and, despite the determined late challenges of Danehill and Exbourne, stayed on relentlessly to claim a length victory over Exbourne with Danehill third.

Newmarket was in uproar. Nashwan, with Carson punching the air in jubilation, returned to a tumultuous reception. Hern doffed his famous panama hat, appropriately ribboned in the blue Nashwan colours of owner Sheikh Hamdan, to acknowledge the cheers. Sheikh Hamdan simply beamed with unconcealed delight. For all of racing this was a day to savour. Hern is a much respected figure and powerful feelings of resentment had been stirred throughout the sport by the Queen

OPPOSITE *Carson powers Nashwan to victory in the 2,000 Guineas*

LEFT *Carson, Hern and assembled Press share a joke after Nashwan's 2,000 Guineas victory in 1989*

and Lord Carnarvon's insensitive treatment of the trainer. Now pent-up emotions could be allowed to run free. The spirit of the hour was typified by the young Newmarket trainer Willie Jarvis, who dashed excitedly about the jostling mass of humanity in the winner's enclosure with tears coursing down his cheeks.

Carson, more than most, could claim a great victory, and not simply with Nashwan. As the arguments raged about West Ilsley, Carson had been prominent in his support of Hern and his staff. Carson was unwavering and vociferous against influential forces in his loyalty to Hern. Racing, at all levels, understood the depth of his commitment to fighting what he saw as a grave injustice and fêted his success the more regally because of it. Hern and Carson were not only back at the top in racing, they were riding high on a wave of public approval.

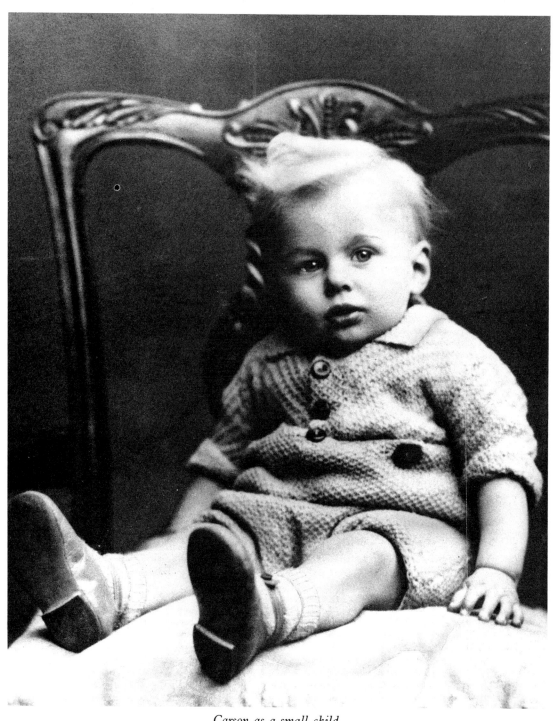

Carson as a small child.
According to his mother, May,
he was walking at eight months

CHAPTER ONE
PAPER TIGER

Stand on the old cobbled bridge over the River Forth as it curls beneath Stirling Castle and you can almost see him now. A young boy, all but obscured by a bag full of newspapers, steers his bicycle out of the chilly half-light to begin the day's round: the eleven-year-old Willie Carson. From the newsagents shop in Cowane Street, run by James Hogg, a former city councillor of Stirling, Carson was responsible for deliveries to Causewayhead, a suburb snaking eastwards on the other side of the river. The route inspired the same tingling dread among his fellow newspaper-boys as a Murmansk convoy; early starts, even by the standards of a paper-boy, made it one to avoid, and those who had to suffer it rarely lasted more than a few months. Carson survived two years. Even now, in the times of his greatest triumphs, he recalls those days with pride. 'If you couldn't say much else about me as a kid, at least I was a good newspaper-boy,' he affirms.

William Fisher Hunter Carson was born in Stirling on 16 November 1942, a 'Son of the Rock' as those from the city are colloquially known. He inherited his curious middle names, which have become as readily identifiable with him as his broad grin and cackling laughter, from an uncle who became a missionary in America. Carson was always called Billy as a child; only later was he re-christened Willie by the media.

His background was solid working class. His father, Tommy, was a warehouseman for Fyffes bananas in Stirling; his mother, May, had a job as a waitress. They worked hard to provide a good start for the children – Billy and a younger sister, Elizabeth. These were trying times; Billy was born during the Second World War and, even long after hostilities had ceased, would feel the privations of continued rationing. Money was never plentiful, but it is unfair to say he was raised in anything approaching poverty. Carson never forgot the sacrifices made by his parents. When his career blossomed he made sure that they, and Elizabeth, were able to move south with him.

He scaled a respectable 6½ lb at his first weigh-in, but both parents are small – indeed May is little more than four feet nine inches tall – and Carson was soon lagging behind his contemporaries in stature. So great was the disparity becoming that Mrs Carson began to worry about how her son would manage in the world. Tommy invested in a pair of boxing gloves and gave the young Billy lessons in self-defence. Their fears were unfounded. The trademark Carson determination was forged early as he built a fierce self-reliance. Bullies who, seeing the tiny youngster, thought they had fastened on to easy prey, were swiftly and painfully disabused. He tried to avoid trouble, but when it sought him out bigger assailants were usually sent packing beneath an unexpected torrent of blows.

Carson is not the only Son of the Rock to have been instilled with a fierce desire to succeed. Billy Bremner, a member of the powerful Leeds United football team of the seventies and captain of Scotland, is also a native of Stirling. So too is Richard Quinn, who, like Carson, would go on to be a Classic-winning jockey. Bremner, who is the same age as Carson, remembers the Stirling of their youth. 'It is a great

Carson receiving the freedom of Stirling together with Billy Bremner. Carson's parents are on the right

historical centre, similar to York in England. There is the castle and an old town, with a real sense of tradition about the place. The town isn't that big but you couldn't really call it a quiet place. There were always plenty of visitors around, particularly during the summer. The industry in those days was based on the mines, and there was a big John Player cigarette factory in the town.'

Carson and Bremner never met as children, but were to be guests of honour at a civic reception in Stirling once established in their respective careers. Carson, never one to miss a photo opportunity, leapt on to Bremner's back and proceeded to 'ride' him, much to the amusement of Bremner's footballing colleagues. Bremner, displaying the reverse of his fiery on-field nature, took the jest in good part.

Tommy and May saw their son's future in a less belligerent use of the hands than he was sometimes forced to employ. Carpentry was high on their list of prospective careers for the youthful Carson. But his size, at first a drawback, was to become his greatest asset. Carson's fellow pupils at Riverside School had long, and not always mockingly, pointed to his becoming a jockey. 'Eleven are you, Titch? And that small? Ha. Have to make you a jockey.' So the chorus ran, time and again, until the idea began to take hold.

One fateful August day the film *The Rainbow Jacket* came to the Allanpark Cinema in Stirling. This 'seasonably sunny tale of the turf', as described by the film critic of the Stirling Observer, told of the rise of a young boy taken under the wing of a warned-off former jockey and guided to Classic success. The film's appeal is not hard to understand. Much of it was filmed at Doncaster, Sandown Park and Newmarket, painting an evocative picture of life on the racecourse and in training yards: the paddock scenes, the excitement of the track as punters scramble amongst the bookmakers, the horses at exercise emerging from the early-morning mists. Even Sir Gordon Richards, fresh from his sole Derby win on Pinza the previous year, made an appearance. '*The Rainbow Jacket* had a lot to answer for,' Carson was to say later. 'It was a film about a young kid coming good as a jockey and it pointed me in the right direction. I made up my mind to be a jockey and spent all the money from my paper round on learning to ride.

'Obviously my size helped. If I wasn't so small I could have ended up knocking nails into bits of wood or slicing up vegetables. I used to enjoy cooking. That was my real interest as a child. I often made the meals at home and my ham and egg pie was something special.'

Carson was well and truly hooked. He returned home and announced to his bemused parents that he wanted to become a jockey. Coming from a boy brought up on the council's Cornton Estate, from a family with no trace of horsey connections apart from Tommy's occasional bet, this was no ordinary request. At the time, May Carson was working as a waitress at the Fourways Restaurant on the outskirts of Stirling. One of the restaurant's customers was Thea MacFarlane, who ran the Scottish Equitation Centre at nearby Dunblane, and the two women began to talk. Mrs MacFarlane agreed to take on the now twelve-year-old Billy Carson, mostly, as she later admitted, as a favour to May, who was being relentlessly badgered by her insistent offspring.

Once a week he would cycle the nine-mile round trip to Dunblane for his ten-shilling lesson, paid for by the twelve shillings and sixpence he received from his paper round. Mrs MacFarlane was staggered to see the tiny figure who arrived. 'So small and with big blue eyes. Too frail for a jockey, and so quiet – not the outgoing character he is today,' she remembers.

He was an almost eerily quiet child, preoccupied with his dreams, anxious to leave for home as soon as the lesson was over. Nor would he be seen in his jodhpurs. The threat of being bullied was his constant companion; to avoid encouraging ridicule he would carry them with him in a bag and change at the riding school. Mrs MacFarlane would urge him not to be so silly; then she would take another look at the Lilliputian character in front of her and decide that he was probably right.

But Billy Carson – and Mrs MacFarlane has never called him anything else – proved an apt and unflinching pupil. He watched and learned as she drummed into him the basics of a classic seat. She never lifted his stirrups or tried to impose a jockey's style; they would be grafted on later if he joined a stable. 'I concentrated on the things that were in my range,' she says, rather modestly, simply encouraging him to give the horse an inch or two more rein as his confidence grew.

His first mount was Jill, a chestnut mare of eleven hands, shrewdly purchased by Mrs MacFarlane for £4 from a band of gypsies. The gypsies believed the mare would be of no use to a riding school, but Mrs MacFarlane disagreed. Her judgement was impeccable. After Jill had been examined by a vet and given the all-clear, she was broken in and became a model schoolmistress for children at the riding school.

Billy and Jill proved largely compatible, although like most relationships it had its sour moments. She sometimes threw him, usually at pace as she negotiated a corner and her young rider went shooting off the side. 'A right little bitch she could be,' Carson was to recall rather ruefully later. 'She always seemed to be going a hundred miles an hour when she ran away with me and I hit the ground.' Again, his resolution was unshakeable. He would simply pick himself up, remount and carry on with the job in hand. No horse was going to defeat him. Carson graduated to a grey mare called Wings, but the message was still the same. He was going to be in control and for that he, not Wings, was going to be the boss.

But Mrs MacFarlane's gift was far greater than an introduction to the simple mechanics of riding. She gave him his chance, the opportunity to express himself on horseback. She would shout and yell in one breath, mother and encourage him in the next. In return, she saw more than simply a pupil beginning to grasp the rudiments. She saw the right attitude, a confidence and an uncomplaining courage which she was determined to support. She saw somebody who one day might just make it. It was why she wrote to dozens of trainers telling them that she knew a lad who maybe had what it takes. Would they give him a chance?

Three had openings for an apprentice: Captain Gerald Armstrong, George Boyd

*Willie dressed in the jodhpurs he wore
while learning to ride at the Scottish Equitation Centre
in Dunblane, near Stirling*

*Captain Gerald Armstrong, whom Carson joined
as an apprentice in 1959*

and Pat Beasley. For all his enthusiasm, Willie knew little about racing and nothing about his three potential employers. He was only fifteen and was facing a major decision for one so young. The day came when it could be delayed no longer; as he sped out of the house on his way to school his mother demanded an answer. After a mental 'Eeny, meeny, miny, mo' as he was later to describe it, a decision was reached: Captain Gerald Armstrong. Not for a single minute did he regret the choice..

Willie Carson arrived at Captain Armstrong's Thorngill stable, some three miles from the centre of Middleham, North Yorkshire, in the winter of 1959. Armstrong, a former officer in the 5th Lancers, ran his yard on army lines: discipline, hard work and absolute integrity were his watchwords. He lived by them and expected no less from his staff. Armstrong taught from a persuasive combination of pedigree and experience. His father, Robert Ward Armstrong, had begun training in the north at a precocious sixteen years of age; for the next sixty-nine years, until his retirement in 1950, he continued to hold a training licence, first near his native Penrith and then after moving to Middleham in 1923.

Captain Armstrong also had a wealth of experience on which to draw. He had ridden more than a hundred winners as an amateur, including a treasured victory for the King on Whitehead at Ripon in 1934, before a serious fall put paid to his career in the saddle. Turning to training, he added several hundred more successes, notable among them Sailing Light's win in the 1953 Lincoln Handicap. He knew his craft, and he had the gift of being able to explain its complexities.

As Carson settled into the realities of stable life, any lingering golden images from *The Rainbow Jacket* swiftly evaporated. The stern regime of long days in an unfamiliar environment tested Carson almost beyond endurance. Homesickness was beginning to gnaw remorselessly at him. During the first year he wrote home regularly, pleading to be allowed to return to Stirling. His mother stood firm. She had encouraged him in his riding lessons and paid for clothes to equip him for his new job. Besides, a contract had been signed for his apprenticeship and it would be honoured. He was staying.

Even with the law laid down to him, Carson struggled to shake off the temptation to throw it all in. 'If someone had come up with a worthwhile idea for me I would have jumped at the chance. Luckily, no one did or I may have joined the rest of the unemployed.' Perversely, his lack of academic skills proved his salvation. 'I was very ordinary, run of the mill, in some ways lazy,' he says. With little else to offer he had no option but to persevere.

One escape route from the daily drudgery for the stable lads was to make for nearby Darlington. Here was excitement: coffee bars, dance halls and the chance to meet girls. All the opportunities a boy could wish for to spend his hard-earned 2/6d a week.

Despite the hard school of stable routine, Carson's natural reticence was to give way to the bounding dynamism that has become his life's trademark. His youthful chirpy vitality and impish looks were an appealing combination; nor were they lost on the local girls. One young lady friend became pregnant and by 1962 Carson had become the father of a daughter. Although he never acknowledges his daughter's existence, he unhesitatingly paid maintenance until her sixteenth birthday. As he says: 'When you're young you make mistakes, but I've done everything by the book. I've paid my dues.'

He was soon to find a more permanent relationship. In the Green Tree coffee bar, a favourite local haunt, he met Carole Sutton; he was nineteen, still labouring in the stables, she was sixteen and attending secretarial college. Carole recalls: 'I was very young when I started seeing Willie, we both were. And, of course, he was so small. When I took him home my mum would say "Shouldn't that little boy be home in bed?'' It became a standing joke. He looked like a younger version of Tommy Steele. He always used to have his hair forward like the singer; he was ebullient, always outgoing when I knew him. Bags and bags of confidence. In that respect he hasn't changed.'

Carson's career was by now beginning to progress. Armstrong, though a hard master, had warmed to Carson's infectious enthusiasm. The trainer would readily spend time with anyone he thought responsive, and in Carson he, like Mrs MacFarlane, found a keen disciple. Carson has never denied the debt he owes Armstrong. 'Whatever style I have it is Captain Armstrong I have to thank for it,' he says. 'He was tough, always driving me on, but I suppose he must have seen something in me. There was no time for a quick five minutes' sleep during the afternoon in that yard. He would have you straddling a wooden bench or a stack of straw with a bridle tied to one end and the reins in your hand. He would stand there shouting ''Push lad, push the way you've been taught. Push, push, push''.'

There, in Middleham, the Carson style was minted. Head down, arms pumping as his mount is powered onwards in a fury of controlled aggression. Not perhaps the silk-smooth style of the natural horseman; rather the grafting, urgent technique of the workman. Effective, though.

Carson's first ride in public was on the three-year-old filly Marija, trained by Gerald Armstrong, at Redcar in May 1959. Styled somewhat grandly as W. H. Carson – jockeys are rarely known by more than one initial – and riding at a gossamer-light 6 st 11 lb, he finished a distant fifth of six runners in the seven-furlong Apprentice Handicap.

An undistinguished start; but he had begun to add practice to riding theory, learning as, over the next three seasons, he put together a collection of rides around the small northern tracks. Yet that elusive first winner was as far away as ever, until Carson was introduced to the three-year-old Pinkers Pond, a brown colt sired by Neron out of the mare Ballyturn. Pinkers Pond's background was some way removed from the top drawer. Neron's finest hour had been to win the Queen Anne Stakes at Royal Ascot in 1951, but Ballyturn had only a solitary win in a selling race to her name in four years of racing. But to Willie Carson, aspiring jockey, he might have been Pegasus.

Whatever heights a jockey may reach, he always holds dear the moment of his first winner. Most come in forgettable races on forgettable cards, cherished down the years only by those closely involved. Carson's first day of glory was no different. The form book records the bare fact that on 19 July 1962, at Catterick Bridge, a course not far from Middleham, the three-year-old Pinkers Pond, ridden by W. Carson, won the seven-furlong Apprentice Handicap by six lengths from Distance Enchanted; Carson's memory, even some thirty years and thousands of winners later, lovingly paints in the human details, the day still sharp and sweet.

'Pinkers Pond was trained by the gov'nor, Gerald Armstrong. I was into the fourth year of my apprenticeship by then, and I'd had twenty-two rides, just screws, really rubbishy horses. Pinkers Pond was disappointing, but he had won a small race as a two-year-old. Charlie Brown, the travelling head lad, had stirred the horse up the day before. He wasn't doing his best, and when jockeys can't make them go, stables put up an apprentice. They always seem to go faster for an inexperienced rider. Pinkers Pond had worked well with two other horses. I'd been told if I could hold him I'd get the ride at Catterick. I did, only just, but I knew it was the chance of a winner so I was trying extra hard.

'The big day came, typically Catterick, overcast and a feeling of damp I couldn't shake off. But it was exciting, my stomach was full of butterflies. The hardest part was holding him on the way to the start. We'd put blinkers on and he was taking a tug. In those days it was the barrier tape at the start, not stalls like it is now. That was a worry. Getting away was maybe twenty-five per cent of the race, and if you got it wrong it was pretty well over before it had started. But I had some experience, so at the off I just kicked him in the belly and sent him on his way, never to be seen again. We made all the running and nothing ever got near enough to give us a race.

'We'd won! What a feeling. Absolutely fantastic, everyone was very happy for me. I revelled in it, which of course you must. Any jockey only rides that first winner once and you never get quite the same feeling again.

'I started with Mr Armstrong on 2/6d a week and by then I was up to 10/6d. Twenty years old and earning 10/6d, so I didn't have a lot of money to go out and celebrate. But it was my first winner, and a start.'

A start, but a sedate one. The victory, so important to Carson, had passed unnoticed by the rest of the racing world. Indeed Carson was to be given a swift lesson in the sport's bitter truths. Flushed with success, he kept the ride on Pinkers Pond for the colt's next race, three weeks later at another Yorkshire course, Pontefract; they finished ninth of the ten runners, barely within telescope range of the winner.

A few more rides trickled in before the end of the season, but none could add to Pinkers Pond's win. 'Even with that first win behind me I wasn't at all convinced I was going to make it,' Carson recalls, 'so I didn't take riding that seriously.'

Gerald Armstrong retired at the end of the 1962 season and sent Carson to his brother Sam's stable at Newmarket. Gerald Armstrong died in 1979, only months after Carson had won his first Derby on Troy. He always took great pride in Carson's achievements and in the fact that it was he who gave Carson his start in racing. As he always reminded visitors, he may never have trained a Derby winner, but he did train a Derby-winning jockey.

Carson swiftly discovered that Sam Armstrong's regime was not for the faint-hearted either. 'I was told I was going to stay and that was that,' Carson remembers. 'In fact he wouldn't let me go home for Christmas until I'd signed the indentures.'

Carson had good reason for wanting to spend Christmas at home. Carole was pregnant, and in January 1963 they married. But he would go alone to Newmarket, to continue his career in new surroundings a long way from home.

CHAPTER TWO
A HARD SCHOOL

Sam Armstrong, the younger brother of Gerald, had been a trainer since 1924. Like Carson, he had spent time in Middleham before moving to Newmarket, first to Warren Place and then to his own yard, St Gatien Stables. Armstrong was a shrewd trainer of horses and men. He was also an astute businessman in an era when many trainers relied solely upon the aristocracy for support. Change was in the air, and he had the wit to see it coming. He cultivated owners from all walks of life, from all points across the social spectrum and from anywhere on the globe. His only criterion was that they had a horse to send him.

For the Maharajah of Baroda he saddled Sayajirao, at that time a record-priced yearling at 28,000 guineas, to win the 1947 St Leger and Irish Derby, and the following season saddled the same owner's My Babu for a 2,000 Guineas success. Towards the end of Armstrong's career, Petingo, owned by the Greek shipping magnate Captain Marcos Lemos, was an outstanding advertisement for his skills. Petingo was the leading two-year-old of 1967 and finished second to Sir Ivor on the following year's 2,000 Guineas. Armstrong was also adept at plundering the big handicaps; few escaped his notice.

His touch in nurturing young riders was no less sure. Josh Gifford, later a champion National Hunt jockey, Paul Tulk, Wally Swinburn and Kipper Lynch were among the talented apprentices to pass through Armstrong's hands. Armstrong had a rule never to take on an apprentice who had previously been with another trainer. Making jockeys was hard enough, he believed, without having to unravel bad habits they had brought with them. But in Carson's case he made an exception, perhaps out of family loyalty, or because Gerald had assured him that here was a boy with a future.

'Gerald told me Carson was a good lad, definitely above average,' Sam was to say later. 'He told me it would be a crying shame to let him drift out of racing.'

Carson had to move into digs in Newmarket alone as Carole stayed with her parents to await the birth of their first child. Tony was born in May, and in July they too moved to Newmarket. By the time Carole and Tony were ready to join him in Newmarket, he had scraped together £50 to put down on a caravan. 'It was more of a mobile home really,' Carole says. 'Willie's parents helped us to buy it. I liked

Tommy and May a great deal, got on very well with them. They were always extremely generous to us.'

They lived first at Red Lodge, five miles out of Newmarket on the Norwich road, and every morning Carson would either hitch a lift from passing motorists or cycle to the yard. After a few months of travelling, Carson decided the time had come to grasp the nettle. He screwed up his courage and asked Armstrong whether he could move the mobile home into a paddock at St Gatien. Armstrong agreed, although as Carson vividly remembers: 'You should have seen his face when that huge thing was towed in.'

Apprentices always knew when Sam saw something in them: he would work them harder than ever. 'He was really tough with me,' Carson says. 'Always pushing and

The 21-year-old Carson with his presentation whip as Evening Standard *Apprentice of the Month*

hard. Nothing came easy. Yet when I look back Sam Armstrong took good care of me.'

Carson's career was hardly moving at breakneck speed but he had at least edged into second gear. He rode five winners in 1963, including Tico, whose victory in a small race at Bogside in Scotland still produces a wry smile.

'The race didn't last much more than a minute, but it took me three days to get up to Scotland and back. I was travelling mostly by train then and on the return journey I had to grab a few hours' sleep in the waiting room at Peterborough station. That wasn't unusual for those northern meetings. I'd drop off in the early hours with nobody around and wake up surrounded by commuters. It was so embarrassing to sit there with everyone staring at me as though I was a tramp.'

As his brother had, Sam Armstrong fashioned an academy built on discipline. There was no room for self-expression; adherence to the house rules was everything. Lads wore caps when riding out (this was in the days before crash helmets became compulsory) and hats when leading up horses at the races; apprentices would not be allowed to use whips until they had ridden five winners, instead being taught to use their hands to bring out the best in their mounts, and each evening they would report back to Armstrong to describe how they and their rides had performed.

Armstrong had little yellow cards typed to lay out each day for his apprentices. 'It seemed like our life was on those cards,' Carson says. 'How to ride the track, what train we were on or who we would be getting a lift with, how to get home, how to ride the horse, everything you could possibly want to know. Then there were other instructions on how to stand outside the weighing room in case a spare ride came, and the final order to report back to him. We all found that the later you left it the more easy going he was. If you went round on the dot of 6.30 you'd get a bollocking if you'd ridden three winners or three losers. Waiting until he'd had a few drinks was a better bet.'

Early in 1964 Carole became pregnant again, with a second son, Neil, and the need for more living space became pressing. They moved into a tied cottage, owned by Armstrong, in Croft Road on the opposite side of Newmarket. 'Two up, two down and an outside toilet,' Carole says. 'But we were gradually moving up.'

Moving up in the world perhaps, but lack of mobility on the ground was proving a handicap. 'We had no transport so we decided it was time to buy a car,' Carole relates. 'We managed to get a Mini on HP, but that exhausted our money. We literally

Carson, still an apprentice, winning on Solennis at Windsor in 1964

couldn't afford to put petrol in it. So I went out and took an Avon round. I went door-to-door on a bike selling cosmetics and that made enough money to keep the car on the road.' The car was much more than just a means of getting around. With transport at his command, Carson was in a position of rare power. He was not about to let the opportunity slip. 'Willie would pick up the other lads from the Armstrong yard and take them roller skating in Cambridge,' Carole says. 'He would charge them for the trip and then bring them back to our house where I would make them all supper, eggs and bacon, or whatever was going. Then he'd charge them for that too.'

Despite Carson's sharp eye for the main chance, money remained tight. As a promising apprentice his salary had risen to £5 14s a week, but that was meagre enough with a growing family to feed and clothe. 'It was tough, but you lived to it,' Carole says. 'Our only luxury, if you could call it that, was a television. We rented it for about ten shillings a week. Really we had to, because it was our one link with sanity. There are only so many things you can do sitting in night after night. All we seemed to do was play cards. Willie was madly competitive even at that. He had to win; he couldn't stand coming off second best. If we could get a babysitter we would occasionally get out to the local hop, but that was rare. No, a social life was no problem – we didn't have one.

'It was hard for both of us. Willie would come back from the likes of Liverpool in the days when they had Flat racing as well as jumpers. He would get back at two in the morning and I would be washing his breeches ready for the next morning. Early morning too, because they still had to ride out before going to the races.'

Difficult though life was, under Armstrong's expert eye Carson became increasingly polished, and more successful. In 1964 he rode fifteen winners and then thirty-seven in 1965, including a first big-race winner when Monkey Palm, trained by Armstrong, took the Great St Wilfrid Handicap at Ripon. 'Now I'd hardly even think about winning a race like that,' says Carson, 'but it was very important to me then.'

That year also produced another milestone for Carson. An apprentice's progress is often judged by how quickly he loses his claim, the right of an inexperienced rider to claim a weight allowance against senior jockeys. Although Carson's growth had been nothing more than steady, he was now on the verge of losing his claim, by now down to 3 lb.

The day did not pass without dramas. 'I was at Redcar to ride Regal Bell for Sam, but I was keen to take the ride on a horse called Patel, trained by Herbert Blagrave, in an earlier race. I needed one winner to lose my claim and Sam knew that as well as anyone. "You've got to ride mine, and if Patel wins you won't be able to claim the 3 lb, so you're not riding Patel," he said. Naturally Patel won, and so did Regal Bell, by ten lengths, so my claim wouldn't have made any difference anyway.'

There is a maxim in racing that apprentices all too often find life becoming difficult when they lose their claim. Carson laid that to rest immediately. The following day he won the opening race at Brighton on Polairia, his first ride without an allowance.

He was beginning to make a name for himself, and as his winning totals grew, so did his self-belief. During his apprenticeship, Sam's son, Robert, later to take over St Gatien and become a successful trainer in his own right, sometimes drove Carson to meetings. As they returned from Thirsk in Yorkshire, Carson having completed a double, he confided quietly to Robert: 'I might just make it as a jockey, you know.' Carson has never ceased to recognise the significance of that moment. 'That was the first time I'd really admitted it to myself,' he says. 'From then I decided to take it more seriously, because I thought maybe I could make a living out of it. Until then I'd been considering doing other things, becoming a chef or carpenter perhaps.'

As Carson's career began to flourish, he and Carole were again on the move, this time to their own house, a three-bedroomed semi-detached bought for £800. 'Willie's parents have it now,' says Carole. 'I suppose it must be worth about £75,000. But things were getting better for us. Now we could afford a three-piece suite and carpets and curtains.'

The move, however, was to present its own problems. By now Carole had taken over as Carson's agent, booking rides, talking to trainers, studying the form book to decide which horse Carson should ride in which race. But the Carsons were the first family to move to the estate, and they had no telephone, an essential item for any jockey to organise his mounts. Not for the first time, the resourceful Carole came up with the answer. 'The builder was the only person who had a phone connected,' she says. 'So I offered to work for him. Answer the phone, do some typing, just generally act as receptionist. He agreed, and that gave me the use of the phone so I could keep doing Willie's rides.'

They were tough days. 'We were like slaves,' Carson says, 'but it made a man

One of Willie's earliest
big-race victories.
Winning the Rosebery
Handicap on Sir Giles at
Epsom in 1966

of me. I learned about life as well as about riding. I used to get my backside kicked even when I did the right thing, just to keep me in my place.'

Irene Banks, who was Sam's secretary, remembers those days well. 'The lads always had to have clean hands and fingernails. They had to look the part. Things have changed, I know, but then the apprentices had always to be smart. They had to have a tie, and a white shirt that had been ironed. And clean shoes – they had to wear shoes that had been polished. They also had to work hard for their money. I didn't see much of the apprentices – generally only when we paid them. Sam wouldn't have them coming into the office and staying for a chat and girls were not allowed in the yard or to ride out. But the lads were paid twice weekly: two shillings and sixpence twice a week at first and then five shillings. It was cheap labour.'

Carole has her own memories of Sam Armstrong. 'Sam was good, even though he was very, very firm,' she says. 'I used to find him a frightening person in some ways. He once looked into Tony's pram and said he wouldn't make a jockey because his feet were too big – yet all three of the boys went into racing. When one of Sam's apprentices went away, he always had instructions which were typed out on a card. On the top of all these instructions it said that they had to take a hat – meaning a trilby – a mackintosh and a form book. Those were the essentials. No apprentice dare go anywhere without a trilby and a form book.'

One of Sam Armstrong's small tricks in teaching his apprentices was to point out a senior jockey on which to model themselves. For a tall rider like Josh Gifford, Armstrong would recommend Lester Piggott; Carson, a much smaller figure, had had it drummed into him to watch and learn from Doug Smith. It was to prove a remarkably prophetic piece of advice.

Carson gets the better of a desperate finish on Duneed at Sandown in 1966

CHAPTER THREE
'THE DRIVER'S A GONER'

In 1966, Bernard van Cutsem, the British-born son of a Dutch count, was trainer to Lord Derby. Van Cutsem lived up to his aristocratic pedigree: stylish, opinionated and often waspish with anyone considered to have asked a stupid question. But there were no reservations about his ability to train, nor to recognise a good horse. He was a shrewd judge and never afraid to back his assessment with hard cash.

The definitive van Cutsem story always bears retelling. After Old Lucky had landed a spectacular gamble in the Royal Hunt Cup at Ascot in 1974, a journalist offered the time-honoured gambit from press to winning trainer: 'Tell me, Bernard,' he asked, 'what's the plan now?' Van Cutsem considered him with a look of barely concealed distaste. 'That was the plan,' he said icily. It was too. Old Lucky, though clearly a good-class handicapper, could get no closer than third in four subsequent starts that season. Van Cutsem had him tuned to the minute when it mattered, and had the winnings to prove it.

Van Cutsem had, in 1964, leased Lord Derby's historic Stanley House stables in Newmarket. He would not be restricted to training only for Lord Derby, however; he would train for anyone keen to utilise his services. Van Cutsem had inherited Doug Smith as Lord Derby's retained jockey, but by 1966 Smith was in the twilight of an outstanding career. He had been champion jockey on five occasions and associated with a host of top-class horses, not the least of them Petite Etoile, whom he rode to win the 1959 1,000 Guineas.

Retirement was creeping up on Smith, and Lord Derby and van Cutsem had to start thinking about a replacement. The discussion about Smith's successor ranged far and wide over a series of candidates before the list was narrowed to two: Sandy Barclay and Willie Carson. Even at this stage opinions were divided. Lord Derby was keen on Carson, but van Cutsem favoured Barclay, who, like Carson, was a Scot. 'Bernard kept pressing for Sandy,' Lord Derby recalls. 'I was forever going on that Carson was the one I wanted, even though he had never ridden a horse for me. I thought he was a good jockey and I had spoken to several people who assured me that he was also an exceptionally nice person.' Before a verdict could be reached, the dilemma was solved for them. Noel Murless moved to sign Barclay, leaving Carson as the intended replacement. The first move was to sound out Sam Armstrong.

Armstrong was enthusiastic in his support for the move, recommending Carson with fervour: 'At his weight I have never seen a better jockey,' he said, delivering a huge vote of confidence in the young Scot.

With the ground prepared, the time had come to approach Carson. 'I remember being called in by Sam Armstrong,' Carson relates. 'I thought it was another rollicking, but Mr Armstrong told me about Lord Derby's offer. I was told to take a couple of days to think it over. Lord Derby, van Cutsem; I needed two seconds.'

It was a late July evening; Carole was busy hanging out washing as Carson returned home with his news.

'Who do you think will be Lord Derby's jockey next season?' asked Carson.

'That was the plan.'
The archetypal Bernard van Cutsem coup as Old Lucky, ridden by Carson,
wins the 1974 Hunt Cup at Royal Ascot

Willie Carson in 1967

'Doug Smith,' replied Carole. 'Who else?'

'But suppose he was retiring, then who?'

Playing guessing games was too much for Carole at the end of a long day and she said so. Carson explained. Smith intended to retire at the end of next season. He would act as his understudy for a year and then the job would be his. After all these years, he would soon be among the first division jockeys.

All that bothered Carson was that he had never spoken to a Lord before. How would he behave? Would he commit some unspeakable social gaffe? He need not have worried. Although he admitted to 'shaking like a leaf' when he met Lord Derby, he quickly discovered his fears were groundless. The peer, whose ancestor founded the great blue riband of the turf which carries the family name, was an approachable, affable man who wasted no time in declaring himself 'an unashamed Carson fan'.

Although the present Lord Derby has not shown the fanatical dedication to the turf evident in many of his predecessors, his runners have always carried an inherent prestige. His colours 'black, white cap' are among the most instantly identifiable in racing and there is no doubt that, in gaining his confidence, Carson and his career had bounded forward.

The position also carried the use of Falmouth Cottage, the traditional home of Lord Derby's jockey. 'Cottage' is a misnomer if ever there was one. The sixteen-room house in the Snailwell Road in Newmarket was a legacy of an altogether grander age when status, rather than practicality, mattered. But Carson remembers how he and Carole could hardly wait to take up residence. 'We couldn't keep our eyes off the place,' he recalls. 'We kept creeping up Snailwell Road in the evenings, poking our heads through gaps in the hedge to plan what we would do with it when it was ours. It was a miracle we weren't arrested as burglars. When we did move in, all we had was the furniture from our semi-detached house, and that was nowhere near enough to fill Falmouth Cottage. So at first we just had to live in corners until we could afford more.'

Yet the dream was so nearly shattered. Carson ended 1966 with thirty-five winners and duplicated that score the following year when he understudied Smith. After the 1967 season had ended in November, he set out to drive to Darlington to deliver Christmas presents to Carole's family. It had to be done early so that he and Carole could get away for a holiday. They never arrived.

As Carson pointed his new Jaguar, a recent sign of blossoming success, up the A1 the weather began to turn nasty. Fog was restricting visibility, but Carson was not unduly perturbed. Driving had become second nature to him now that he was clocking up 30,000 miles a year, and besides, he was behind the wheel of his new car, one he enjoyed driving. The fog was swirling when Carson saw the grey shape loom out of the mist right in front of him. There had been no lights because the lorry was side-on, its driver attempting a U-turn. In the screeching of brakes and rending of metal, the Jaguar slammed into the lorry.

Carson's recollection of the minutes that followed is distressingly clear. 'I went straight under him, me and the wife and kids. What a mess. I broke my femur; so did Carole and Neil. I also broke my jaw, wrist, needed twenty-seven stitches in my face and head. The wreckage was awful. The front wheel was in the radio, my broken leg was touching my chin, my head was outside, the windscreen gone.

'I was drifting in and out of consciousness, holding the leg because the pain was so bad. When I passed out and dropped it the pain woke me up again. When the police arrived they took my tie off and tied my leg to the steering wheel so it wouldn't move. Then the ambulance came, and the fire brigade to get me out. They had to jack the car apart. I was still drifting, but I heard the ambulanceman say "Look at the driver, he's a goner." I can remember thinking "Not yet I'm not. I'm still here." '

For Carole, too, the day burnt deeply in her mind. 'How could I forget it? Apart from the horror, I still limp to this day. It was a real pea-souper, visibility down to about 20 yards. I was two months pregnant with Ross, our third child. Neil had been sleeping on my lap in the front, but a couple of minutes before the accident I put him in the back with Tony, thank God. The next thing I knew was Willie's lights shining up the side of the lorry and the car disappearing under its back axle. It's ironic, really, that the crash should happen in the best car we'd ever had.'

They were taken to St James Hospital in Leeds. Carson recalls with grim amusement that when he regained consciousness in hospital his first sight was of a priest by his bedside praying for him. The shock put him out again. Next time he came round to hear a Jamaican nurse chanting 'Ten, twenty, thirty . . .'. It was his money she was counting, and joking about how far a couple of hundred pounds would take her. She then put the money away for safe-keeping.

The lives of the family had been saved, but Carson's career was in grave jeopardy. In a matter of months he was due to become Lord Derby's retained rider. How could he ever be fit? It was to be as determined a battle as he had ever fought. This time the prize was too great for failure to be considered.

He was in hospital for three long months before being discharged, his right leg in calipers. Carole's stay was even more prolonged; she would not be released until Ross had been born, some seven months after the accident. Doctors warned Carson that he could not expect an early return to the saddle. But Carson, as a gesture of faith, had promised Lord Derby that he would ride a Derby winner for him, and a horse of van Cutsem's called Laureate was beginning to show distinct signs of Classic promise. Medical opinion suggested that Carson did indeed have a chance of being fit for Epsom in June. The jockey knew he could do better than that.

Laureate, with the Australian Russ Maddock in the saddle, began the season with an easy win in the Union Jack Stakes at Liverpool. At that time the Grand National meeting staged mixed programmes of Flat and National Hunt racing.

As he watched on television, Carson's resolve strengthened. 'I couldn't do anything then,' he relates. 'I still had calipers on my legs. But I saw him win, he just hacked up. He looked a Derby horse and I knew then I had to ride him. So I started doing some illegal work on the leg, at least as far as the doctors were concerned. I took the calipers off, began riding a pony.' Although he could still barely walk, he spent hours in the sauna he had built for himself in the garden as he tried to lose the weight he had put on in hospital. Many more hours of physiotherapy also had to be endured. 'When I next went to the doctor I told him I'd taken the calipers off and got back quicker than I should. But time was getting short and I had to take my chance.'

Carson missed the first three weeks of the season, but astonished van Cutsem by asking to be allowed to ride in the morning gallops. Van Cutsem acceded to Carson's wishes, not wishing to dent the jockey's enthusiasm, but was canny enough to insist that Carson at first rode only the trainer's own hack. A hack is the mount used by the trainer to supervise his string at exercise, and is usually chosen for his equable temperament. A professional jockey, even on his way back from serious injury, would have little difficulty controlling such a horse.

By 16 April, just five months after his near-fatal crash, Carson considered himself fit for action. On the opening day of the Craven meeting at Newmarket, he hauled himself on to the three-year-old filly Bikini for the Elveden Maiden Stakes. Unfortunately for Carson there was to be no fairy-tale ending, as Bikini, an outsider, came home nearer last than first. But he had made his point: he was back. Four days later, at Thirsk, Laureate ran in the Classic Trial Stakes. Although Carson was riding at the meeting, van Cutsem kept Maddock on Laureate, waiting for final confirmation that Carson was back at his best. Laureate was beaten into third behind the northern-trained Chebs Lad, but Carson was to end the day in style.

'One of my rides was one of Lord Derby's for Doug Smith, who had become a trainer since he retired. She was called Hedge Sparrow, a two-year-old having her first run. Really on her toes, the bloody thing dropped me three times. Each time I picked myself up and that told me there was nothing wrong with the leg. A terrific mental boost. I didn't get anywhere near winning with her but I was on the mark with The Pack Horse in the last. That got me going again.'

Carson rode Laureate for the first time in his next start, the Dee Stakes at Chester. After Laureate's disappointing run at Thirsk, Carson decided to take the initiative and try to make all the running. The plan worked perfectly. In front from the off, Laureate ran on gallantly in the short straight to hold off the odds-on favourite Attalus by half a length. It was a great day for Carson; not only had Laureate redeemed his reputation, but he had in the process given Carson his first big-race win for Lord Derby.

Another quickly followed. Laureate was looking like a genuine Derby challenger again, an impression he confirmed with another eye-catching success in a competitive race for the Derby Trial Stakes at Lingfield nine days later. Carson's pledge to Lord Derby could be fulfilled at the first attempt. It was Carson's first Derby ride at the age of twenty-five, a reminder of how slowly his career had developed. Of today's top riders, Lester Piggott had his initial experience of the Derby as a fifteen-year-old in 1951; three years later he won on Never Say Die. Pat Eddery had his first

Winning the Lingfield Derby Trial on Laureate in 1968

Derby ride at twenty; Walter Swinburn won on Shergar as a nineteen-year-old at his first time of asking; Steve Cauthen had already pocketed the American Triple Crown as a seventeen-year-old on Affirmed before he came to Britain. Carson had taken a long time just to be part of the magnificent day, let alone win the race. It is just another small part of his struggle, and there are times when you can see that the memories of it will not leave him in peace.

Laureate lined up at Epsom the fourth favourite at 100–8. Sir Ivor, trained in Ireland by Vincent O'Brien, was the odds-on favourite at 4–5 with Remand on 4–1 and Connaught 100–9. Let Carson tell the story of the race: 'Connaught was a front runner and he was right up there making the pace. I was sitting in just behind him. I could hardly hold Laureate. I looked down the course and I could see the jam stick [the jockey's term for the winning post] and I began to wonder if . . . . Then bang! He stopped to nothing and I was going backwards. It turned out there was something wrong with his heart. That was my first Derby ride – a disaster.'

While Laureate's chance evaporated Connaught set sail for home. Just as it looked as though Sandy Barclay's enterprise may have won the day, Lester Piggott produced Sir Ivor with a devastating burst of speed to cut down Connaught deep inside the final furlong. The finish remains one of the most spectacular to have graced the Derby. Carson, by now little more than a spectator, brought Laureate home a ragged eleventh of the thirteen runners. Carson's verdict on his first Derby ride was a little harsh. He had travelled in hope and Laureate could hardly be blamed for an unhappy physical defect. There would be other Derby days, some better, some worse than this one. Most importantly, he had secured a foothold in the great race; he would not be dislodged now.

By the end of the season, Carson had accumulated his highest score of sixty-one winners, a respectable score considering he had missed the early weeks of the year. He also had the satisfaction of landing another major prize for Lord Derby, the Northumberland Plate at Newcastle, one of the season's most demanding handicaps, on Amateur.

For the next two years, Carson continued to build steadily, amassing sixty-six winners in 1969 and eighty-six in 1970. His success introduced him to an ever-wider audience of owners and trainers, including other patrons of van Cutsem's stable besides Lord Derby. As Carson noted: 'Riding winners builds confidence. Doing the right things in a race begins to come naturally.'

The 1970 season was a watershed for Carson. Not only did his eighty-six winners take him into third place in the jockeys' championship, behind Lester Piggott (162 winners) and Geoff Lewis (135), his highest placing, but for the first time he had more rides (699) than anyone else. The Carson strategy was there for all to see: hard work, travel anywhere to ride, implacable will to win. Bind them all together and winners surely had to follow.

Yet despite his growing success, Carson was still irked by the jockey hierarchy in van Cutsem's stable. He was firmly established as Lord Derby's first choice, but van Cutsem often preferred to look elsewhere for other horses in the yard, especially when it came to the best of them. And these were golden days for Stanley House. Van Cutsem had the magnificent mare Park Top and the high-class middle-distance runner Karabas in his care, but when either of them contested the great prizes it was to Piggott and Lewis, rather than Carson, that van Cutsem turned. As Lord Derby recalls: 'Bernard still put Lester up in the big races or on a really fancied horse. It was one of his stipulations which I told him would never work. I didn't think it was right. Willie would ride in the less important races and then be stood down when the valuable ones came along. I told Bernard that as far as I was concerned I wanted Willie to ride my horses.

'When Bernard wanted Willie to become stable jockey, the situation could have become intolerable. If Willie suddenly found he had a good horse and then discovered Lester was to ride it, that would have been unfair. Anyway, when Bernard did suggest it, I had to tell him that as he had not wanted to come in with us in the beginning he would have to be satisfied with second retainer on Willie while I kept the first.'

It is easy to understand Carson's preoccupation with Piggott. At Sam Armstrong's he had always been vulnerable to Piggott's relentless, far-and-wide sweep for winners; Piggott, besides his professional standing, was Sam's son-in-law and always likely to pick up the plum rides. Now Piggott's shadow had again fallen over him at van Cutsem's. 'There were times when I thought I was doomed to play second fiddle all my life,' Carson complained. But luck was ready to turn against Piggott and smile sweetly on Carson.

In 1971, van Cutsem trained Crowned Prince, a full brother to Majestic Prince, who two years earlier had won the Kentucky Derby and Preakness Stakes, the first two legs of the American Triple Crown. A $510,000 yearling, then a world record, Crowned Prince was as much a media event as a racehorse. Cameras followed his every move and the press could not get enough news on the colt's progress. His jockey, it hardly need be said, would be Lester Piggott.

The public's first view of Crowned Prince was at Newmarket on August 21. In a welter of publicity, he made the most inauspicious start possible. Sent off at 2–7 favourite, he was beaten two furlongs out and crept home a distant sixth to the 33–1 winner Jeune Premier. However, he was soon to show his true colours. In his next two starts he won the Champagne Stakes at Doncaster and the Dewhurst Stakes at Newmarket in the manner of a high-class horse. He was rated the best two-year-old in the country that year.

In 1971 van Cutsem had an Aladdin's cave of two-year-old talent. One in particular, High Top, was of singular interest to Willie Carson. While Piggott, his *bête noire*, was concentrating on Crowned Prince, Carson struck up a fruitful partnership with High Top. High Top's breeding was more plebeian than his illustrious stable companion, and indeed the colt had failed to reach his reserve when offered at Newmarket sales. He was instead bought privately for 9,000 guineas by Sir Jules Thorn. Sir Jules had made an astute purchase. In four starts, with Carson aboard for three of them, High Top was successful three times including a victory in the Observer Gold Cup at Doncaster. Carson shared in the Doncaster triumph, the most significant of the trio of wins. High Top ended the season officially rated just 2 lb inferior to Crowned Prince.

In what was to be a memorable year for him, Carson was also associated with another high-class van Cutsem-trained two-year-old, Sharpen Up. Sharpen Up was unbeaten in five races, the last four of them ridden by Carson, including the Middle Park

Stakes at Newmarket. With Sharpen Up rated 5 lb behind High Top, van Cutsem could claim the remarkable achievement of having three of the top six two-year-olds in the country in his stable, each of them having claimed at least one of the season's leading juvenile prizes.

For Carson, too, it had been a memorable year. His partnership with the top horses was pleasing, but no more so than his second position in the jockeys' title race. He had garnered 145 winners in his best ever year, and although Piggott still held sway he was only seventeen ahead of Carson. Astonishingly, Carson had doubted during the season whether he had the drive to become champion. The figures suggest otherwise: once again he had recorded the highest total of rides during the season (795). Piggott's crown was in range, and Carson, despite public protestations to the contrary, knew it as well as anyone.

But as the 1972 season began, it was Crowned Prince who continued to hog the headlines. He was established as a short-priced favourite for the 2,000 Guineas on the strength of his two-year-old form, and now he had to prove that he had retained that ability as a three-year-old.

Van Cutsem chose the Craven Stakes at Newmarket in April for his reappearance. But, sent off a 4–9 favourite, he was bitterly disappointing. Although he held every chance two furlongs out he was soon beaten, finishing fourth of the five runners. With the colt's Classic hopes in ribbons, van Cutsem decided upon a racecourse gallop at Yarmouth as a last chance. Once more Crowned Prince failed to shine. The trainer was forced to concede the inevitable: 'Crowned Prince will not run in the 2,000 Guineas,' he announced. 'We believe he has a soft palate.' A soft palate hinders a horse's breathing. Crowned Prince never ran again, and was retired to stud in Ireland. With Crowned Prince's departure went Piggott. He had been contracted to ride him, but with Crowned Prince out of the way he seemed to lose interest in van Cutsem's stable. Carson's position was further strengthened when Sharpen Up was also beaten in a Classic trial, the Greenham Stakes at Newbury. From three possibles, van Cutsem was now reduced to just one runner – High Top, the mount of Willie Carson.

The day of the 2,000 Guineas broke cold, wet and miserable. This was Newmarket at its most unwelcoming, rain sweeping across its vast expanses, a pervasive grey dampness seeping into the spectators. But this was High Top weather. He had won his previous race that season, the Thirsk Classic Trial, on soft ground, and any softening in the officially good going would not worry him. He was made the 85–40 favourite, with Vincent O'Brien's Irish challenger Roberto second favourite at 7–2. Piggott's antennae had picked up clear possibilities in the shape of the Bill Marshall-trained Grey Mirage, and he had helped himself to the ride on the 5–1 third favourite.

Carson set out to play catch-me-if-you can on High Top. 'I aimed to make all the running,' he recounts. 'I went straight off, never looked left or right, just stayed in front and let the others try to come to me. They couldn't, and we kept going to beat Roberto. He went on to win the Derby, so it had to be a good performance.

I was delighted to have won it for Bernard. He treated me like a son. We had a banner up at the house welcoming me back. It was a fantastic day and, of course, my first win in a Classic.'

High Top never won again. From four subsequent starts, his best efforts were second places in the Sussex Stakes at Goodwood and the Prix Jacques le Marois at Deauville. However, Carson always believed he was a better horse than he showed, and advised Lord Derby to take a share in High Top when he retired to stud. Lord

Carson's first Classic victory: winning the 2,000 Guineas at Newmarket on High Top, from Roberto, in 1972

Derby acted on Carson's opinion and had no cause to regret it. High Top became a successful sire, with Top Ville, the winner of the Prix du Jockey-Club among his offspring.

'Willie was insistent I should take a share in High Top,' Lord Derby recalls. 'He was proved absolutely correct. Willie thinks a lot about racing and is usually a sound judge. His easy-going, joking image can be rather misleading.'

Encouraged by his first Classic win, Carson set his sights on another landmark: his first jockeys' championship. With Piggott choosing to ride abroad more regularly,

Returning to the winner's enclosure on High Top

the race developed into a battle between Carson and another rising star, Tony Murray.

By the middle of the season, Carson had the edge over Murray and the bookmakers were making him long odds-on for the championship. Then disaster struck. In a maiden race at York in late August, Carson's mount, Tritherm, unseated him. A fractured cheekbone and a cracked wrist were diagnosed, and a badly bruised right eye was there for all to see. Six weeks off was the doctors' verdict. By the time he returned the season would effectively be over. Carson was horrified. The injuries were one thing, but the prospect of losing that championship was something else again. His gloom deepened when, later that day, Murray went on to complete a double, narrowing his lead to four. The news galvanised Carson: he had come too far, worked too hard, to be denied now. He had to fight and beat this setback.

He discharged himself from hospital and, after just a weekend's rest, was back in action at Windsor five days later riding Parnell to a twenty-length victory. Foolhardy his return may have been, but there is no avoiding a sneaking admiration for such courage and determination. How appropriate, too, that Parnell, one of his favourite horses, should be the one to welcome him back. Parnell shared Carson's never-say-die spirit. He had joined van Cutsem from Ireland at the beginning of 1972 and, after winning a handicap and the more important Prix Jean Prat at Longchamp, almost caused one of the sensations of the year when second to the superb Brigadier Gerard in the King George VI and Queen Elizabeth Diamond Stakes at Ascot in July. Only a length and a half separated them at the line but 'The Brigadier' had drifted to his right, into the rails, forcing Carson to switch Parnell to the outside. A lengthy stewards' enquiry ensued but the result was allowed to stand.

'Brigadier Gerard certainly swerved in the closing stages and today I think would have lost the race,' Carson says. 'He didn't truly get a mile and a half; it was only his class pulled him through. Parnell just wouldn't let go of him, he just kept plugging away.'

As the season moved into its final months, Murray had taken on a new lease of life. He was stringing together winners all too frequently for Carson's liking; Carson would again have to draw upon all his reserves if he was to have the last word. Murray, now the racing manager to Tony Budge, one of racing's finest patrons, remembers vividly the struggle over the closing weeks. 'With six weeks to go I was about ten ahead. I was with Ryan Price then, and although I'd had a good run his horses were going over the top. The winners just dried up. I only had one more from the stable.

'I knew then what would happen. Willie's light weight is such an advantage. He could get all sorts of rides that just weren't open to me, so he raced on to win his first championship. It's impossible to overstate the importance of his light weight. He did not have to waste like almost everyone else, and wasting takes an enormous toll, both physically and mentally. It gets to you, and in the last two months of the season you would be completely knackered. Willie meanwhile was walking round with a spring in his step.'

Carson clinched the title with 132 winners, thirteen fewer, curiously, than he had

Willie with his first wife, Carole,
and their three sons in 1973

ridden the previous year. Murray, having striven so doggedly all year, was ten behind in second. Once more Carson had claimed the highest number of rides during the season (829), over 100 more than Murray. This was a triumph to savour, at least when Carson realised the enormity of his achievement. Legend has it that he slept for five days after taking the title, so drained was he by his ceaseless chase for winners. 'I wanted that first championship so desperately,' he says. 'I tried really hard, going everywhere, trying to ride everything. I'd have ridden a donkey in a race.'

Carole shared in the victory. Before Ted Eley became Carson's agent she had booked her husband's rides, learned the form book inside out to advise him on his choice of mounts, and kept the family together as a retreat for him. 'I like to think that I helped him win the championship, not just because I helped him on the professional side but because I took the strain on our personal life. It was left open for him to go ahead and win the championship.'

CHAPTER FOUR
A QUESTION OF STYLE

With his first Classic, a jockeys' championship and more than 600 winners behind him, Carson was now immovably in the first rank of his profession. His riding achievements brooked no argument about his abilities, yet he had varnished the cold statistics with a personal touch: he had become the punters' champion. His all-action, true grit style of jockeyship had endeared him to anyone who had ever risked a shilling on a horse. They knew that to have Carson on your side was to recruit a man who refused to acknowledge a lost cause. Back Carson and you had backed a trier.

Just as Piggott is easily recognisable for his high, backside-in-the-air perch – 'I have to put it somewhere,' he once told a questioner attempting to unravel the mystery of his style – Carson's motif is the short-armed punch, all motion and non-stop aggression. Carson has always been reluctant to believe he even has a style, and, on the rare occasions he does concede the point, likes to keep the discussion simple. He sees no merit in the minute detailing of how he rides, nor does he understand the fascination it holds for others.

'There is nothing complicated about it at all,' he says. 'I am just going with the horse, keeping in time with his motion. Everyone thinks I am doing something but I'm not. I'm riding with him until I push full bore to the line. I certainly don't try to make myself look that way; I'm not even sure I want to look that way. It's not very elegant and in small ways I've been trying to change my style for years. But I can't say it worries me.' Despite his wariness of being dragged into a discussion on the mechanics of his riding, he does concede a preference in tactics. 'If there is a pattern to my riding it is that I like to be up with the leaders most of the way. You often find that just as people think I'm beaten I'll come again and do the business right on the line. As long as the horse has something to give, I will keep going. But it is a matter of experience and feel. There is absolutely no point in carrying on if a horse packs it in.

'I suppose I sometimes make work for myself. I get the horses so relaxed they often have a lot of ground to make up. But their energy is still there, and while it is I keep on pushing until they produce it.' However, Carson is guaranteed to bristle at the suggestion that his manual of tactics has only a single entry. 'People have said that I am all push, kick and wallop,' he once complained. 'I believe I have as much tact as anyone. I don't hit horses much at all. I analyse them, try to work out what goes on in their minds. But I do know that I am not a Scobie Breasley, the type of jockey who is best at bringing horses from behind.'

Carson has always found it difficult to shake off what has become ingrained in the public's mind as a trademark – forcefulness. Even some of the sharpest professional observers fasten on it immediately. Susan Piggott, the wife of Lester and daughter of Sam Armstrong, had married before Carson arrived at her father's stables, but she has followed his career closely both as friend and her husband's rival.

'He is extremely strong and always gets the best run out of a horse,' she says. 'He has tremendous energy, you would always make that point about him. I suppose

Pushing ahead:
Carson showing all his strength and determination

if I were to say that on some horses he was not quite good enough, that would be unfair. His record is that of a very, very good jockey, right up there with the top two or three.'

Mrs Piggott's views are echoed by John Sharratt, recently retired as the senior race reader for *Raceform*, the definitive guide to the running of horses. For almost fifty years, Sharratt watched hundreds of jockeys in tens of thousands of races, noting their strengths and weaknesses. What are the qualities that impress him in Carson? 'He is so strong, powerful and vigorous,' says Sharratt. 'He does not knock horses about yet always seems to draw the last ounce from them. I did not see Joe Childs, who was reputed to be the strongest of the lightweight jockeys, but I doubt there has ever been anyone better at the weight than Willie.

'If you ever had a horse that needed a good kicking or slapping, Willie was your man. You never see him sitting up in the saddle, never see him easing horses up, never see anyone more determined. I have always maintained that if you could drop Willie into the saddle two furlongs from home he would never be beaten.'

Sharratt does, however, voice the same reservation that Mrs Piggott was perhaps too tactful to expand. Intriguingly, he too cites Scobie Breasley, the master of the waiting race, as the antithesis of Carson's raw energy. 'There is no finessing with Willie,' he says. 'It's simply not him. Look at a video of Charlottown winning the 1966 Derby by a neck and you can understand what I mean about finesse; or Lester Piggott on Petite Etoile in the Oaks and Coronation Cup, when basically she did not get the trip. Those were the times when Scobie and Lester would excel. If a jockey needed to bustle one along then Willie would soon have him going. I'm not saying that he couldn't hold one up: he could, he's such a professional. But he has always been about vigour and energy. He preferred to get on with it . . . kick, push, kick, push, that's his style.'

However, Edward Hide, for many years the leading jockey in the north and renowned for a razor-sharp tactical brain, argues that Carson is a natural horseman. 'Horses just run for him,' is Hide's view. 'He had Ted Eley booking his rides for him and he would turn up in the weighing room, ask me what the race was, how far it was and who was in it! He was an instinctive rider. He would invariably put himself in the right place at the right time. He always seemed to give himself the opportunity to make the right decision, and, of course, more often than not he did. I don't think he ever studied the form book. Willie could subconsciously take things in; he would remember how a horse ran last time and how it needed riding this time. It's odd because he seems to be looking down the horse's neck and not where he's going. Perhaps the fact that he has always had so many rides each season has given him an extra feel for what horses want as individuals.'

Eley, who also acted as chauffeur for Carson, quickly noted a habit which helped the jockey maintain his edge. 'His secret was that he could sleep absolutely anywhere,' Eley relates. 'I used to wake him in the morning and run a bath for him. He would then fling his clothes on and jump in the car. By the time I had driven from Falmouth Cottage to the clock tower in Newmarket, a matter of a couple of hundred yards, he would be asleep. Then he would wake up when we reached the track and say "Oh, we're here are we?" '

Alan Amies, a colleague of Sharratt's at *Raceform* and also vastly experienced, sums up the appeal of Carson the jockey. 'It is always tremendous to watch him at York or Doncaster, or any track with a long straight. You see him looking for room, just nudging his horse, setting one up that he really fancied. Then he would get his head down and go for the line and you knew that that was it – or it generally was, anyway.

'You can always see when Willie fancies his chances; that is why the punters love him so much, because he is always working hard. Punters like to see that, don't they? I remember at Pontefract one day when he was riding a long odds-on favourite – 1–10 I think – and even then he couldn't sit still. He kept changing his hands and pulling his whip through; it won so easily and yet he just could not sit still.'

The traits of Carson the jockey reflect Carson the man: determined, boundlessly driven, single-minded in pursuit of his goals. No matter with whom you speak, the story is the same: Willie as a man on the run, searching for the next ride, the next winner. 'If he couldn't excel at it he wouldn't do it, whatever he attempted,' Carole, his first wife, says. Eley, too, has felt the ferocity of the flame at close quarters. 'If Willie had been a boxer,' he says, 'he would have been world champion for ten years.'

Whatever his style, it worked. Carson was again champion in 1973 with 164 winners and came close to adding to High Top's Classic success. The day of the 2,000 Guineas at Newmarket was almost identical to the previous year: chilly, blustery and uncomfortable, but this time Carson was not on the favourite, as High Top had been, but an 18–1 outsider, Noble Decree.

Noble Decree was owned by the American oil magnate Nelson Bunker Hunt, who would end the season as leading owner thanks principally to Dahlia's win in the King George VI and Queen Elizabeth Diamond Stakes. Noble Decree, trained by Bernard van Cutsem, had also once promised great things. He ended his two-year-old career with a win in the Observer Gold Cup at Doncaster when, ridden by Lester Piggott, he had beaten Carson's chosen mount Ksar, also trained by van Cutsem, by half a length. For Carson, it seemed, there was no escaping his shadow. Noble Decree, the top-rated colt of 1972, had disappointed on his first outing of the new season and, with punters tending to consider a horse as only being as good as its last run, had gone to Newmarket largely unfancied. In a field of eighteen the betting was dominated by overseas challengers. The Irish-trained Thatch, and Targowice, from France, headed the market at 5–2 and 11–4, first and second favourite respectively. No member of the home team was quoted at less than 10–1.

With Piggott on board Thatch, Carson was reunited with Noble Decree. Prolonged rain during the morning had turned the going yielding, which was in Noble Decree's favour. As the race developed, there was a moment about a furlong out when history looked like repeating itself. Carson, all determination and power, forced Noble Decree to the front, overhauling the 50–1 outsider Mon Fils. But, for all Carson's driving, Mon Fils would win the day. Given a no less inspired ride by Frankie Durr, Mon Fils edged ahead close home to seize the verdict by a head.

Van Cutsem's decision to run Noble Decree in the 2,000 Guineas left him free to deploy Ksar as his more probable Derby representative. Ksar was living up to that hope. He won Classic trials at Kempton and Lingfield, and was steadily growing in stature as a possible Derby winner. However, van Cutsem then decided to run Noble Decree in the Derby. Carson would have to make the choice which one to ride. It was an early test of Carson's judgement of the form book as it applied to the big races. He decided on Ksar.

As the betting public mulled over Carson's choice, ten days before the race the jockey was kicked on the way to the start in a minor race at Warwick. For a few

Carson with his chief retainer, Bernard van Cutsem, in 1974

days his participation in the race hung in the balance. But after a concerted course of treatment he was able to return two days before Epsom to confirm his fitness. He had no problems, but opted to miss the following day to be absolutely right for the Derby.

The Derby that year attracted a far from memorable field. No fewer than twenty-five runners went to the post, with steady support forcing Ksar down to 5–1 favourite. The public had fastened on to Carson's choice and they were backing his belief in the horse with hard cash. Sadly for Carson and his band of followers, it was not to be. Although he had indeed made the right move in siding with Ksar, they could do no better than fourth behind Morston, the mount of Edward Hide. Noble Decree, who injured his back in running, finished last but one. Curiously, Hide had been van Cutsem's choice to replace Carson if the injury had proved serious, and had indeed been booked by the trainer if Carson failed to make it. When it became clear that Carson would be fit, Hide was free to switch to Morston. In that strange quirk of fate, he as much as anyone had reason to appreciate Carson's remarkable powers of recovery.

Willie receiving his William Hill Golden Spurs Award as Flat Jockey of the Year in 1974. Fred Winter (right) won the National Hunt Trainer Award

While he was stable jockey with van Cutsem, Carson had also forged valuable links with two rising young trainers, Clive Brittain and Barry Hills. Indeed, Brittain would later credit Carson with helping him to get the best possible start. 'He threw himself heart and soul into getting behind me,' Brittain says. 'He never stinted himself, and that goes for Carole too. They both kept encouraging me and helped to bring new owners into the yard at a time when I needed all the support I could lay my hands on.'

Carson was also involved, somewhat unwittingly, in bringing in Brittain's most important patron, Captain Marcos Lemos, the Greek shipping tycoon. 'Captain Lemos had horses with Bernard van Cutsem when Willie was stable jockey for him,' Brittain says. 'The Captain had a thing about one of them, Averof; he just didn't think that Willie and the horse got on together. This put Bernard in an awkward position. He had the champion jockey and didn't want to undermine him by taking him off the horse. But he also had an owner who was unhappy with the situation, and, of course, equally entitled to his opinion. The three of them, Willie, Bernard and the Captain, sat down and talked the position through, and it was decided that Averof should come to me.

'He turned out to be a top-flight miler and won good races at the Derby meeting and Royal Ascot. It was all part of Captain Lemos buying Carlburg Stables in Newmarket and setting me up as resident trainer. Naturally, it was a wonderful decision as far as I was concerned, but I think there was something else that was important about the move. It came down to men of principle who were prepared to take time, discuss their differences and respect each other. That was getting on for twenty years ago, and I think the game's lost something in that time. Now I feel that type of situation would end in argument and bickering, rather than mutual agreement.'

Having been instrumental in bringing in Lemos, Carson, by accident, also nearly drove out another owner. 'I rang Carole to ask if Willie would ride one for me at York,' Brittain relates. 'This horse, Argutus, was an absolute so-and-so. It would get up on its hind legs and walk for fifty yards before it came down, then up it would go again. It was slow too. In its previous race it had finished about two furlongs behind everything else. Carole laughed and told Willie that I had a certainty for him. So when I saw Willie at York I told him he was in for a tough ride, but just to keep pushing away and hope for the best. I'd told the owner that I wasn't at all hopeful and not to bother backing him.

'Well, unfortunately, the breeder of Argutus, Major Poyser, had seen that Willie was riding and assumed this was going to be the day. So Argutus was backed in from 33–1 to 9–2 and looked like a shrewd gamble. It must have been one of the worst races ever run. The horse was doing nothing, but Willie kept pumping furiously and got up right on the line to win. Not surprisingly, the owner was furious. He thought I'd deliberately discouraged him to get a better price for myself and threatened to take his horses away. He had eighteen in the stable and this was 1972, when I was still trying to find my feet. I couldn't afford to lose him. But I told him the story and he kept the horses with me. You certainly couldn't fault Willie for trying so hard, and only he could have got it home. He gave it 110 per cent. But it would have been ironic if one of his greatest efforts on my behalf had cost me a major owner.

'Funnily enough, no sooner had I finished my explanation to the owner than Major Poyser was on the phone asking me to take a couple of horses. He'd had a fortune on Argutus and thought I was a genius.'

Although one of Brittain's clearest memories of Carson is of him pushing away at Argutus, he believes it is unfair that Carson should be accused of only being able to ride a horse one particular way. 'Of course people always mention his determination and driving style, but they forget he has a shrewd racing brain to go with them. Willie knows exactly what he is capable of and can size up a race to outsmart jockeys who think he is only going to do one thing. He's a magician; there's no one who would leave Willie behind in a battle of tactics.'

Carson's long-time friendship with Barry Hills – Hills had been sitting alongside Carson as the jockey watched on television while Laureate won at Liverpool – was also burgeoning professionally. Hills had employed Carson on a regular basis since

Carson (left) on the gallops at Lambourn with the trainer Barry Hills

he began training in 1969, and the association was enjoying growing success. In 1974, Hills trained an attractive chestnut filly by Aggressor called Dibidale. She had finished second once in two races as a two-year-old and began her three-year-old career at Haydock with Lester Piggott in the saddle. She started an odds-on favourite, but in a driving finish was edged out by Carson's mount, Scientist.

Hills recalls the day clearly. 'Lester came back and told me Dibidale was no good. But I still believed in the filly and asked Willie to ride her in the Cheshire Oaks

51

*Willie rides Dibidale bare-backed after the saddle slipped
during the 1974 Oaks. They finished third
but were disqualified for failing to carry the correct weight*

at Chester, which was a harder race than the one she'd just lost. Willie sent her off in front and she won easily. From then on she became his ride.'

The next objective was the Oaks, for which she was the 6–1 third favourite behind Polygamy and the Queen's Escorial, ridden by Piggott. The key to Dibidale was her need for soft ground, but just twenty-four hours before the race the signs were that she would be out of luck. The ground at the Surrey course was firm, which would give Polygamy, trained by Peter Walwyn, an edge. Both Hills and Carson have vivid recollections of what would prove to be one of the most fateful days in the history of the great race. 'I flew up to Haydock to spend the night with Robert Sangster,' Hills says. 'I knew the ground was against her and I was praying for rain. During the night it started, and I lay there wondering if it was the same at Epsom. I couldn't wait to get up the next day. At five o'clock I telephoned John Sutcliffe, who trains at Epsom, and asked him if the weather had been the same. When he told me it had, I was more confident. At breakfast that morning, everyone was getting their bets on. We flew down to Gatwick in Robert's plane with Nick Robinson, Dibidale's owner. It was a rough old trip, but at least the weather was in Dibidale's favour, even if it wasn't doing much for us.'

Carson too was well aware of the filly's going preference. 'We were right in the middle of a dry spell,' he remembers. 'Then that night the rain started, pitter pat, pitter pat. Barry was delighted, but I knew Walwyn wouldn't be. The ground eased enough for us to run her.'

As the race turned out, the ground proved to be the least of Dibidale's, and Carson's, problems. Let Carson tell the story. 'About six furlongs out, around halfway, her head seemed to be getting further away from me. It was as though her neck was growing longer. Then it dawned on me that the saddle was slipping. The problem was that she had a big front but it rather tapered away. Between the six and five furlong poles I was beginning to think there was something wrong. Then the shock hit me, that I was becoming unstable. It was only my balance keeping me on. I was getting to the buckle end of the reins, just sitting there thinking about my future. Here I am, in the Oaks, I look like riding the winner and all the time my saddle's slipping. Any sharp movement and I'm a goner. I thought the most important thing is to keep a good rhythm. I took hold of her mane and put my feet right at the end of the stirrups. Two furlongs out I decided the time had come to abandon the saddle and jump onto her back. Then I realised I could still win and started to ride a finish − it never occurred to me about the weightcloth. She finished third but should have won.

'Tony Murray helped me pull up and it was a relief to get off her back. It was then that I thought about the weightcloth and just threw my whip down in frustration. When I got back to the weighing room the clerk of the scales said "Weigh in, Carson". I had to ask him "What with?" '

Victory went to Polygamy, but Carson would not be dissuaded that Dibidale had been the moral winner. That view was borne out when she gained the more concrete reward of an impressive victory in the Irish equivalent at the Curragh, with Polygamy a well-beaten third. She also went on to collect the Yorkshire Oaks on her only other start in 1974. But she never won again, and the ill fate which dogged her at Epsom returned to claim her life the following season. In the Geoffrey Freer Stakes at Newbury she broke her off fore pastern and had to be put down. She is buried at Hills' South Bank Stables in Lambourn. It was as though a family curse had

Friends and rivals. Willie Carson and Pat Eddery at Wolverhampton in 1974

reappeared to haunt Dibidale. Her granddam, Priddy Maid, had been involved in the death of jockey Manny Mercer, whom she threw on the way to the start of a race at Ascot in 1959. Mercer was killed instantly.

Carson ended 1974 with 129 winners but now the jockeys' championship had become the property of the brilliant Irishman Pat Eddery, who would take the crown for four consecutive years as stable rider to Peter Walwyn's spectacularly successful Lambourn stable.

The 1975 season was to be a fateful one for Carson. Towards the end of the year Bernard van Cutsem, his employer and mentor, died after a long illness. Carson, having been loyal to van Cutsem in the face of the trainer's declining number of winners as poor health took its toll, was now without a retainer.

He concluded the season with a respectable 131 winners, the more so in view of van Cutsem's health problems, but was again overshadowed by Eddery. Carson did, however, forge a successful relationship with the delightful filly Rose Bowl, trained by Fulke Johnson Houghton. The daughter of Habitat took the Queen Elizabeth II Stakes over a mile at Ascot and followed up in the prestigious Champion Stakes at Newmarket.

With Carson now without a retaining stable, Hills approached him with a view to Carson riding for him. But before any deal could be put together fate again took an interest in their association. Carson rode Solitary Hail to win the Granville Stakes at Ascot, a race for two-year-olds which had not previously run, but they were then beaten by Wollow in the more important Champagne Stakes at Doncaster.

Vernons Pools boss Robert Sangster, the owner of Solitary Hail, wanted Carson replaced. 'Robert was doing his year or two out of the country and kept hearing that Willie was making mistakes,' Hills says. 'He wanted Piggott on Solitary Hail the next time it ran and that was that. Being jocked off is always unpleasant for any rider and it hurt Willie. That put paid to any idea of him becoming my stable jockey.'

Carson could have been forgiven a sly grin as Solitary Hail was well beaten on his next start, the valuable Observer Gold Cup at Doncaster. With Hills effectively ruled out of the race for Carson's services, Clive Brittain moved swiftly to secure Carson as his stable jockey for the 1976 season.

Carson is pulled from his mount, Pericet,
by striking stable lads at Newmarket in 1975

CHAPTER FIVE
'A MAN WHO FIGHTS TO WIN'

On Coronation Cup day in 1976, the Thursday of the Epsom Derby meeting, Dick Hern and Lord Porchester, the Queen's racing manager walked into the press box. That two such establishment figures should take the unusual step of asking for the press's attention suggested that something was afoot, an impression confirmed by the air of gravity surrounding both men. We soon had the answer.

It was Hern who spoke. 'From next year Willie Carson will be my stable jockey,' he said. 'He will replace Joe Mercer.' The bald announcement seemed to echo round the room like a pistol shot. Mercer, 'pipe-smoking' Joe, was much admired in racing, and the prospect of his being unceremoniously shown the door was not easy to absorb. Mercer's rhythmical, driving style of riding was a textbook in action. More than any other jockey, Lester Piggott included, he was cited as the man aspiring riders should copy. His technique owed much to his elder brother Manny. Manny, in his turn, had been taught by another supreme stylist, Charlie Elliott.

Joe Mercer had ridden for West Ilsley for twenty-three years. For Jack Colling, Hern's predecessor at the stables nestling at the foot of the Berkshire Downs, he had won an Oaks on Ambiguity and been associated with such marvellous stayers as Hornbeam and Master Of Arts. When Hern took over West Ilsley in 1963, having been champion trainer the previous year from his Newmarket base, he swiftly forged a powerful alliance with Mercer, who continued to ride for the yard. St Leger victories on Provoke and Bustino were complemented by a 1,000 Guineas victory on the Queen's Highclere.

There was also Mercer's association with Brigadier Gerard, universally acknowledged to be one of the outstanding racehorses of the twentieth century. Hern and Mercer took 'The Brigadier' to seventeen victories from eighteen starts.

The dismissal of Mercer, the Queen's jockey as he was generally described in contemporary reports, was a major issue. Even *The Times* carried the story on its front page. Nor was the timing particularly appropriate. Only a day earlier Mercer had ridden the Hern-trained Relkino into second place in the Derby behind Empery. 'I was told last year that one of Dick Hern's owners was not happy with me,' said Mercer, 'but I am heartbroken it should end this way.'

Now Mercer had been sacked in favour of Carson, cast by the press in the role of usurper. It was a bitter pill for many to swallow. 'Whatever happened to loyalty?' was the question which was guaranteed to make an appearance in every discussion on the subject. But loyalty had never been an issue to the owners of West Ilsley: Sir Michael Sobell and his son-in-law Sir Arnold Weinstock (now Lord Weinstock). They had bought the stables from Sir John Astor and were determined that they should be run with an eye to business. The family owned the yard and most of the horses, and they saw it as their prerogative to appoint whichever jockey they wished. Even the Queen, a long-standing patron of Hern's, had little alternative but to go along with the appointment.

To Sir Arnold Weinstock, Mercer's removal was primarily a business decision.

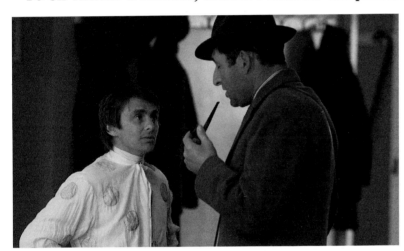

Carson and trainer Dick Hern: they would quickly forge a formidable alliance

In the same way that he guides the electronics giant GEC, Lord Weinstock evaluated the situation and acted accordingly. At the time of the announcement Mercer was forty-one, Carson only thirty-three. To a man planning for the future there could be just one outcome. 'It was long-term thinking,' Lord Weinstock told me in his office overlooking Hyde Park. 'By signing Willie we could look forward to another ten or fifteen years with him riding for us. I would admit that neither the timing nor the way the news came out was ideal, but circumstances rather pushed us into it. Joe had known for a long time that his contract would not be renewed, but around the time of the Derby he came to us to find out for certain if that was still the case. It was then that it all came out.'

But the inimitable Carson style had already caught Lord Weinstock's discerning eye while Mercer was still stable jockey at West Ilsley. 'We had a runner, Straight Flight, at Glorious Goodwood and I was watching the race on television. I thought we had a fair chance, and going into the final furlong we were in front and going well. Willie was at the back of the field on a grey horse, apparently beaten. Then all of a sudden he got his mount running and drove it in front right on the line to beat us. I thought it was quite a performance. This was the kind of man I wanted, one who fights to win. That attitude would suit us and he would come fresh to the stable.'

The race Lord Weinstock recalled was the 1974 Gordon Stakes when Grey Thunder, an unconsidered 25–1 outsider, was powered home by Carson to catch Straight Flight, ridden by Mercer, in the dying strides. It had indeed been a virtuoso performance of never-say-die jockeyship, and, perhaps prophetically, had sown the seeds for Carson to beat Mercer in an altogether bigger contest. Although Lord Weinstock's official reason, that Carson was the man for the future, was largely true, there was another more personal ingredient. Mercer had become almost immovable in his near quarter of a century at the Berkshire yard. He had partnered all of the stable's top horses and knew every blade of grass on the gallops; when he gave his views on a horse's merit, no further discussion was allowed.

Even today owners are sometimes treated with scant regard by trainers who, to a large extent, are inclined to treat the horse as their personal property. The media, it should be said, are far from blameless in encouraging that attitude. Constant references to 'Michael Stoute's colt' or 'Henry Cecil's filly' cannot help but render owners invisible. However, at least matters have moved a long way from the days of Fred Darling, whose owners, should they have had the temerity to arrive unannounced, were peremptorily ordered to take their animals elsewhere.

Mercer's standing hardly rivalled the autocratic Darling, but he still carried too much sway for a man as independent and strong-willed as Lord Weinstock. Apart from anything else, it took a deal of the fun out of owing racehorses. 'If Joe said a horse would never win again, that was it,' as Lord Weinstock put it. 'It became a non-conversation because there was nothing more anybody could add. It wasn't a question of being pro-Willie or anti-Joe, but I must say that I do get on better with Willie.'

While the press continued its criticism of Lord Weinstock and Sir Michael, Mercer

Willie with Lord Weinstock, the owner responsible for Carson joining Dick Hern

and Carson played out the remainder of their respective contracts. Neither was to end the season without incident. Carson's decision to join West Ilsley had stung Marcos Lemos, his current employer. Lemos first heard the news on television and maintained, not unreasonably, that he should have been told privately in advance. 'I imagine that Joe must have wanted a decision,' Lemos was to say later, once the dust had settled, 'but Willie must have known what was going on as well. He kept silent when he might have told me what was happening.'

Although Carson and Lemos have long since buried any disagreements, at the time Lemos could not shake off his irritation at the way Carson's move had developed. With three weeks of the 1976 season remaining, Lemos severed Carson's contract. At the Newmarket Houghton meeting, on 16 October, Carson was booked to ride Lemos's three-year-old colt Derringo in the Highflyer Handicap. Derringo, a handicapper of some ability, but far from remarkable, finished sixth in a race for which he was quoted by the bookmakers at 6–1. Lemos, unhappy with what he believed to be a lack of effort on Carson's part, decided they should part company. The irony was not lost on a jockey whose dynamism had become recognisable throughout racing. 'Of all the things I could have been fired for,' he said. 'Usually people criticise me for trying too hard.'

The impending move had also come as a major disappointment to Carson's friend and, through Lemos's patronage, retaining trainer, Clive Brittain. 'When the announcement came it wasn't a great surprise but obviously it was a setback for me,' Brittain says. 'We were having a good year together. I thought something was in the air but Willie had been sworn to secrecy and couldn't tell me. It must have been a difficult situation for Willie. He's so loyal and honest and he wouldn't have liked not being able to let me know what was happening. But he'd been asked not to and he went along with that.'

Carson ended the season with 138 winners, a slight increase on his previous two years' totals but still well short of prising the title away from Pat Eddery. Rose Bowl was again a force, winning a second Queen Elizabeth II Stakes at Ascot and only narrowly failing to add a second Champion Stakes to her resumé. She was beaten a neck by Vitiges, trained by Peter Walwyn and ridden by Eddery.

Mercer, too, simply kept going about his business. In his last season at West Ilsley, one of the two-year-olds he rode was the Queen's Dunfermline, a daughter of the Derby winner Royal Palace. Although she failed to win in her three starts she twice finished second in high-class company at Doncaster and Ascot. Her pedigree suggested that she would be suited by at least a mile and a half as a three-year-old but Hern, conscious that she would have to improve before she could be considered Classic-winning material, was worried about her habit of laying back her ears and putting her head up at the finish. When he suggested that blinkers might help her concentrate, Mercer was adamantly opposed. 'Don't do that,' he said. 'It's only a sign of inexperience.' How right he was, and what a legacy that advice would leave for Willie Carson.

CHAPTER SIX
JUBILEE CELEBRATION

Willie Carson's career can be divided into two halves: the years before and after he joined Dick Hern. The partnership began in 1977, the year of the Queen's Silver Jubilee. The timing was in itself a cue for a fairy-tale beginning, and we were not to be disappointed. Carson had inherited the promising royal runner Dunfermline among Hern's crop of three-year-olds. Her three races as a two-year-old revealed

Willie Carson in 1977, a great year for him

her potential, but Hern had been keen not to ask her to do too much in her first season. Patience and more patience were the qualities which created lasting success with racehorses. 'It is vital not to overtax a two-year-old's strength,' Hern would repeat endlessly. 'One hard race at that stage can jeopardise its future career.'

Dunfermline wintered well and the race chosen for her reappearance was the Pretty Polly Stakes over ten furlongs at the Newmarket Guineas meeting. She had no trouble winning comfortably. Carson opted to ride her for stamina and, sending her into the lead fully two and a half furlongs from home, he had only to push her along to beat Olwyn by four lengths. Despite the authority of that success, Dunfermline never captured the public's imagination for the Oaks. Her chance was considered much inferior to that of Durtal who had won her reappearance race, the Fred Darling Stakes at Newbury, in a common canter. Even Carson was lukewarm about Dunfermline's prospects. 'I said she was no good,' Carson recounted later. Ted Eley, his former agent, spent fifteen years with Carson and has vivid memories of that summer. 'Willie never rated her,' he says. 'He used to call her a big, ugly filly. But I liked her. I backed her for the Oaks and put her in a double with Hot Grove, his mount in the Derby.'

Carson came to the Derby meeting with two respectable if not outstanding chances. Hot Grove, trained at Blewbury near Didcot, by Fulke Johnson Houghton, had been an easy winner of the Chester Vase, usually a sound guide to the Derby. But the talking point of the race was the French-trained miler Blushing Groom. He was an outstanding horse, but would he stay the extra half a mile? There was also the inevitable Lester Piggott, this year on The Minstrel, from Vincent O'Brien's Ballydoyle stable in Ireland.

Piggott had ridden Hot Grove at Chester and looked for a while as if he might continue the partnership at Epsom. But, after exercising his usual brand of brinkmanship, he finally opted for The Minstrel, third in the English 2,000 Guineas and then runner-up in the Irish equivalent. 'You run him and I'll win on him,' Piggott muttered to O'Brien.

When racing fans talk about Piggott's greatest rides, his performance on The Minstrel that day is always near the top of the list. Yet Carson too rode a magnificent race. His game plan was to exploit Hot Grove's stamina, and he did it with a vengeance. He seized the initiative three furlongs out and, head down and arms working like pistons, went hell-for-leather for the line. Piggott and The Minstrel went in pursuit. Through the final furlong he demanded everything The Minstrel could give, and the chestnut never faltered. Piggott threw in everything: strength, a unique feel for the Epsom camber, a will to win so strong you could almost reach out and touch it. Carson, too, was at his driven best: punching away on Hot Grove, keeping him running, drawing the last ounce from him. But it was to be The Minstrel's day. He wore down Hot Grove, stride by inexorable stride, until he overhauled him, as the *Timeform Annual* would so eloquently put it, 'in the shadow of the post'. Hot Grove was beaten by a neck with Blushing Groom, whose stamina had indeed failed him, another five lengths away third.

Sport, no less than life, is so often about winning, and in the race's aftermath Carson received little credit for his imagination and endeavour. He, after all, had lost. Yet a more realistic assessment of both riders' performances can be made by studying the subsequent efforts of the victor and vanquished. The Minstrel added the Irish Derby and King George VI and Queen Elizabeth Diamond Stakes to his Epsom spoils. Hot Grove could manage just one more win during the remainder of the season, when he beat comparatively modest opposition in the St Simon Stakes at Newbury.

Johnson Houghton, disappointed at being denied a Derby win but delighted with

Hot Grove's run, said simply: 'Both men were inspired. Willie nearly stole the Derby on a horse who was several steps below top class, but no other jockey alive could have won on The Minstrel. If Lester had been sitting in the stands, Hot Grove would have won the Derby.' Pat Eddery, a prolific collector of champion jockey titles, was on Night Before, who had to be pulled up after breaking a blood vessel. He, too, has nothing but admiration for Carson's display. 'Willie rode the perfect race that day. It was just unfortunate for him that they met The Minstrel, who was a bloody tough horse, and Lester got the best out of him. He went on to beat me and Orange Bay in the King George the same way. He stuck his head out, determined he wasn't going to be beaten. There aren't many horses who would have got past me that day.'

While Carson had to lick his wounds over that defeat, he at least had Dunfermline to look forward to in the Oaks. Piggott would again be his greatest rival as the rider of the strongly fancied Durtal. As the race approached, Durtal was a short-priced favourite. But disaster struck. Nervy and constantly on the move in the paddock, she bolted on the way to the start. The saddle slipped, and the huge crowd watched in horror as Piggott was dragged along the ground before being shaken free. Durtal collided with the rails, gashing herself badly enough not only to be withdrawn from

RIGHT *An inspired Lester Piggott on The Minstrel (left) just pips Carson on Hot Grove in the 1977 Derby at Epsom*

OPPOSITE *Winning the 1977 Oaks on Dunfermline by three quarters of a length from Freeze The Secret*

the race, but to be off the course until the autumn. Ironically, Durtal was trained by Barry Hills, who, three years earlier, had suffered the miserable ill luck of Dibidale's saddle slipping in the Oaks.

In the re-formed betting market Triple First, Michael Stoute's Musidora Stakes winner, was made favourite in front of Mrs McArdy, the 1,000 Guineas winner, and the French challenger Jalapa. Dunfermline was only 6–1, a reflection of the betting public's apathy towards her.

The market bore little relation to the race. Entering the final two furlongs, Vaguely Deb and Freeze The Secret, both trained by the up-and-coming young Italian Luca

Cumani, were disputing the lead, with Dunfermline attempting to challenge but apparently starting to struggle. The situation was tailor-made for Carson. He went to work, coaxing, punching, cajoling, thrusting and making certain that the filly's abundant stamina was brought into play. The Oaks seems to demand even greater stamina of its participants than the Derby, even though it is run over the same course and distance, and it was only in the final strides that Dunfermline edged in front to beat Freeze The Secret by three-quarters of a length.

Carson was ecstatic. The image remains of him, standing up in the irons, whip aloft, a mile-wide grin splitting his face. And why not? He had carried off a hugely popular public victory in his first season in a new job. He was entitled to celebrate. 'The greatest day of my life,' Carson said. 'To ride a Classic winner for the Queen in Jubilee year is something you hardly even dare dream about. My only regret was that I'd had an idea about winning and trying to get a little flag off someone to carry as I rode back. It might have been frowned upon but it would have been the perfect ending. I was a very proud man that day; I'm a royalist, you see, I love our heritage.'

Dunfermline's win also helped seal what was to become an outstandingly successful relationship between Hern and Carson. As Ted Eley says: 'They had this tremendous rapport. Willie had been too familiar with Clive Brittain and before that too frightened to say a word to Bernard van Cutsem. Willie needed someone he could respect and he found that in Dick Hern.'

Royal Ascot, some two weeks after the Derby, was disappointing, as West Ilsley failed to register a winner. But at Glorious Goodwood, another of the great festivals of British racing, it was a different story. Goodwood is one of Hern's favourite and most successful meetings. Dick and Sheilah Hern take a house at West Wittering where they can relax and entertain friends. The Major loves nothing better than a good sing-song, and his enthusiastic rendition of *Won't you come home Bill Bailey* is guaranteed loud applause.

A winner for the stable was invariably followed by the evening ritual of Dick and Sheilah walking on the beach, where the trainer would trace a picture of horse and winning post in the sand. Since his accident, Hern watches from his wheelchair while Sheilah does the honours in the dusk.

In 1977, although Relkino, one of the stable's stars, could finish only third to Artaius in the one-mile Sussex Stakes, Hern still had to make two pilgrimages to the beach. On the Thursday, Carson drove Tobique to a decisive victory in the William Hill Southern Handicap for Lady Beaverbrook, the owner of Relkino; the following day, wearing the same colours, Carson was again at his forceful best when winning the Dandizette Handicap on Topbird.

Artaius's brilliant pillar to post victory in the Sussex Stakes was symptomatic of the pattern of the season. Vincent O'Brien had plundered the top British prizes with an armoury of top-class horses. As well as Artaius and The Minstrel, O'Brien had despatched Be My Guest, Godswalk and Solinus to collect valuable races. His statistics for the season make remarkable reading: from his County Tipperary base he won just eighteen races in Britain, yet such was their importance he finished the season as champion trainer with £439,000 in prize money. Hern was his closest pursuer, but despite a good season in which he won seventy-two races, he was still more than £100,000 adrift of O'Brien.

The story of owner Robert Sangster's association with O'Brien during the late seventies and early eighties was one of the most colourful episodes in the history of the European turf. Together with O'Brien's dynamic son-in-law, John Magnier, they revolutionised the concept of stallion promotion. Horses were not bought simply to win races: they were bought to win the big races and so maximise their value as stallions.

Sangster provided the money, O'Brien the training genius and Magnier the stud management and financial expertise. Nor was Lester Piggott's assistance in the saddle to be sneezed at. It was O'Brien who crafted the blueprint for the operation. His success with the Triple Crown winner Nijinsky had opened his eyes to the suitability of the offspring of Northern Dancer, a top-class racehorse and influential sire, for racing on European grass tracks. Each summer, at the Keeneland Yearling Sales

Carson stands up in the stirrups on Dunfermline as
he wins the 1977 Oaks at Epsom for the Queen from Freeze The Secret

(Gerry Cranham)

ABOVE *Carson and Troy win the 200th Derby in 1979 by an astounding seven lengths*
(Gerry Cranham)

RIGHT *Henbit (spotted colours) gives Carson a second successive Derby victory in 1980, despite fracturing a cannon bone a furlong from home. Master Willie was second*
(Gerry Cranham)

ABOVE *Sun Princess leaves the opposition trailing in the 1983 Oaks* (George Selwyn)

LEFT *The outsider Petoski (nearside) runs on strongly for Carson to overhaul Oh So Sharp (No. 15) in the 1985 King George VI and Queen Elizabeth Stakes at Ascot* (Gerry Cranham)

RIGHT *Carson returns to a crowded winner's enclosure on Don't Forget Me after winning the 1987 2,000 Guineas*
(Gerry Cranham)

BELOW *Carson drives out Don't Forget Me to beat Pat Eddery on Bellotto in the 1987 2,000 Guineas at Newmarket*
(Gerry Cranham)

LEFT *Carson and Lady Beaverbrook celebrate with champagne Minster Son's victory in the 1988 St Leger at Doncaster*
(George Selwyn)

BELOW *Minster Son, bred by Carson, wins the 1988 Gordon Stakes at Goodwood*
(Sporting Pictures)

ABOVE *Prince Of Dance
and Carson (far side)
dead heat with Scenic in
the 1988 Dewhurst Stakes
at Newmarket*
(George Selwyn)

RIGHT *Nashwan, one of
the greatest horses Carson
has ever ridden, winning
the 2,000 Guineas at
Newmarket*
(Gerry Cranham)

ABOVE *Carson's spectacular dismount from Nashwan after winning the 2,000 Guineas*
(Gerry Cranham)

LEFT *Willie gives Nashwan a victory kiss after their great triumph in the 2,000 Guineas*
(Gerry Cranham)

RIGHT *At the line
Nashwan is a clear
winner* (Gerry Cranham)

BELOW Nashwan asserts
his superiority in the
1989 Derby
(Gerry Cranham)

at Lexington in Kentucky, he would scour the catalogue for desirable recruits, and his unerring eye for a horse made sure that he found some.

The next objective for Artaius would be the Benson & Hedges Gold Cup at York's August meeting. Hern was keen to take him on again with Relkino, despite Artaius looking impregnable. The bookmakers saw the race as a foregone conclusion: Artaius was the 8–11 favourite, Relkino a 33–1 outsider. But it was Hern who was proved right. Relkino's four lengths defeat of Artaius was one of the sensations of the season. There was no semblance of fluke about the result: Relkino won fair and square. Here Carson was to find a curious quirk in the perception of victory and defeat among the press. Having been only narrowly defeated in the Derby, but virtually ignored, he had now scored a famous victory and again found himself ignored. Hardly a word of praise could be wrung from the newspapers. Headlines screamed 'Artaius mystery', 'O'Brien baffled' and other nonsensical interpretations of the race. Nobody was interested in why Relkino had won, only how Artaius had contrived to lose.

Carson maintained a discreet silence, but Hern, remarkably for a man whose wariness and distrust of the press was legendary, produced a stinging reply. I had telephoned him some days later simply as a routine check on matters at the stable, but the mention of Relkino produced an angry response. Hern interpreted the reaction of the press in failing to give Relkino's win its due as tantamount to a slur on his reputation. It had not happened by chance, he insisted, but by careful discovery of what made the previously unpredictable Relkino tick.

As a three-year-old the previous season, Relkino had run a fine second to Empery in the Derby, but his subsequent efforts were so disappointing that he was branded a rogue. Nothing could have been further from the truth. Relkino's problem had been that he pulled far too hard for his own good and so had exhausted himself before the finish of the race. In an attempt to find the key to Relkino by controlling him through his mouth, a Citation bit was tried, but to no avail. However, before the Sussex Stakes Relkino was galloped in a double-mouthed snaffle, which has two bits, the joints of which are slightly offset and make it difficult for the horse to lean too heavily on it. The answer had been found. Unable to lean too hard on his bit, Relkino became more manageable. At Goodwood he settled beautifully for Carson, running on well over a distance too short for him. Over an extra two and a half furlongs at York, he was fully entitled to run a good race. And he did.

Barely had Carson weighed in after Relkino's victory than he was off to the paddock to team up again with Dunfermline in the Yorkshire Oaks. However, after excelling on Relkino he was caught on the hop on Dunfermline. The race was run at a slow pace, precisely what such a stamina-laden filly did not want, and she was caught flat-footed when Pat Eddery dashed Busaca into the lead about half a mile out. Eddery's opportunism won the day and Dunfermline was left to come home a rather ragged third. Carson, however, preferred to believe that his previous low opinion of Dunfermline had been vindicated. 'I told you she was no good,' he told Eley with some satisfaction. 'You were dead lucky to collect at Epsom.' Eley stood between the two camps on Dunfermline's defeat. 'I certainly didn't agree with Willie that she wasn't good enough,' he says. 'But I wasn't sure either that it was Willie's fault she had been beaten. I thought it was down to her own shortcomings, that she had to have a strongly run race to show her best form.'

With a true test of stamina a necessity, the obvious target was the St Leger, run over 1 mile, 6 furlongs and 127 yards at Doncaster in September. Once again, Hern and O'Brien would be in opposition, and once again O'Brien would provide an apparently unassailable odds-on favourite. Alleged was his name, and he was as low as 4–7 for the St Leger after an impressive win in the Great Voltigeur Stakes at York.

Where The Minstrel, by now retired, had been O'Brien's choice for the great middle-distance prizes of summer, Alleged had been groomed to carry that mantle in the autumn. But for all Alleged's power and quality, many at West Ilsley were prepared to bet that Hern would have the last word. Eley had already backed Dunfermline, and Brian Procter, the chief work rider, was growing in confidence.

Dunfermline wins the 1977 St Leger at Doncaster after an epic struggle with Lester Piggott and Alleged

Carson tries on the St Leger cap for size

'Dunfermline worked really well before Doncaster and I thought she would win the Leger,' Procter relates. 'Then a friend of mine, a very sound judge of racing, telephoned me and said that he thought Dunfermline would win the St Leger, but Alleged would win the Arc.'

It was an absorbing conundrum. Hern, determined there would be no repetition of the dawdle at York, decided to run a pacemaker, Gregarious. But, even if she returned to her best, would Dunfermline be good enough to beat Alleged? Hern was in no doubt that Carson's role was vital. 'She could pull very hard and Willie

*Dunfermline is led into the winner's enclosure
after the St Leger*

had to get her to settle,' Hern says. 'But her trump card was stamina. She had won the Oaks by staying and she would battle all day and not give in.'

Carson was the right man for the job. When Gregarious folded up half a mile from home having set a strong gallop, Piggott sent Alleged to the front. But Carson was alive to the move and stuck like a leech to the favourite. A furlong and a half out, Carson played his hand. He drove Dunfermline, now in full flight, ahead and, digging deep into his indomitable will to win, kept her there. Only in the last few strides did Piggott bow to the inevitable and allow Dunfermline to forge a length and a half clear at the line. But the principals had come close together and a stewards' enquiry was announced. For twenty minutes everyone on the course held their breath before the result was allowed to stand. 'The race suited me,' Carson said. 'He made a lot of the running and I was able to come out from behind him. There was only me could go with him.'

Willie with a young admirer, dressed in the Queen's colours, outside the weighing room at Newbury in 1977

Alleged and Dunfermline were to meet in the Prix de l'Arc de Triomphe at Longchamp the following month but, over the shorter trip of a mile and a half, Alleged was the victor. Dunfermline was fourth, beaten just under four lengths. 'I tried to do the same again,' Carson said, 'follow Alleged and then go past him. But it didn't work. I got trapped and couldn't get out when I wanted. By the time I did get some room it was too late.'

Whatever Carson's problems (and he was not helped by an injury to Gregarious which robbed him of his pacemaker), Piggott was at his imperious best. He dictated the pace and when he struck for home poached enough of a lead for Alleged to come home without having to face a serious challenge.

Dunfermline was to have one more race that season, a return to France for the

Prix Royal-Oak, run over one mile, seven and a half furlongs, at Longchamp late in October. But by then she had had enough and could finish only third to Rex Magna.

Apart from Dunfermline, Carson's principal money-spinner in 1977 was Boldboy. Lady Beaverbrook's remarkable old servant had raised his game to new heights at the age of seven. So unmanageable was he in his younger days that he had been gelded at the end of his two-year-old career; Boldboy had subsequently raced with such zest and enthusiasm that he had established himself as a firm public favourite. During Carson's magnificent season, he rode the gelding to victory in five of his nine starts. His triumphs included the Sanyo Stakes at Doncaster and the Challenge Stakes at Newmarket, both for the second time, and the Vernons Sprint Cup at Haydock.

What a year it had been for West Ilsley, though. Carson had come through his first season as stable jockey to Hern bathed in the glory of two Classic winners for the Queen in her Silver Jubilee year. Although he was unable to wrest the jockeys' title back from Pat Eddery, he could justifiably congratulate himself on a clear second with 160 winners, sixteen behind Eddery. More importantly, he had sealed a relationship with Hern which would serve both men well.

While one professional relationship was blooming, another personal bond was being officially severed. In November 1977, after fourteen years of marriage, Carson and Carole were divorced in an uncontested case, just days short of his thirty-fifth birthday. Carson's view 'that we just grew apart' is not that much different from Carole's. 'We had plenty of good times,' says Carole, who has since married Chuck Spares, the former trainer. 'Willie thought that I was not as ambitious as him and didn't want the same things out of life. He said as much in a magazine interview, which annoyed me at the time. But looking back I think he was probably right.

'I used to go on trips abroad with him during the winter but I was never really that keen on leaving the children. Although racing is my life I prefer the other side of it, keeping an eye on the results rather than going to race meetings all the time. Perhaps I just did not fit into that mould. We married too young and just drifted apart. I can't say it was a particular woman who split us up. Suzanne Kane was the symptom, not the cause. If it hadn't been her it would have been someone else. She just lasted longer than the rest. There's no bad feeling between us; in fact I get on well with Suzanne.'

Whatever the rights and wrongs of the divorce, Carson has never failed to acknowledge the enormous part played by Carole in his climb to the top. As much as anything, she gave him stability in the early days, just as he was beginning to make a name for himself. 'Being wed so young, I stayed closer to home than most,' he says. 'I was never bothered by the spivs who try to get hold of young jockeys when they start to make the grade. I also had three tough bosses who stopped me from becoming swollen headed . . . Captain Gerald Armstrong, his brother Sam, and Carole.'

Suzanne Kane: 'The secret of being happy with Willie is being able to accept that racing is his first love, and any woman must come second'.

CHAPTER SEVEN

'HE'S THE BOSS'

Carson's divorce came as no surprise. His relationship with Suzanne Kane, whom he had met when she worked as a stable girl at Barry Hills's stable in Lambourn, was an open secret.

As early as 1974 the gossip columnists had unearthed the romance and remorselessly pursued Carson to Hong Kong, where he was riding during the winter. Suzanne had jumped the gun by professing her love for Carson, despite the fact that the jockey was, at least as far as the public were aware, happily married. Carson was furious when Fleet Street tracked him down. 'I am not in love with her,' he said. 'She should not have said those things. I am angry and very surprised that she came out with that.'

He also admitted to having discussed the situation with Carole in a telephone conversation. 'She was bloody livid,' he said. 'She hung up on me after five minutes.' Then added, somewhat sheepishly, 'I did most of the listening.' It was one of the rare occasions when a woman had the last word with Carson. Carson's bewilderment was less than frank. He had known Suzanne for a year previously, when he was riding regularly for Hills and she was nursing an ambition to become an amateur jockey. Although she never attained any great prominence as a rider, Suzanne did win races, the credit for which she swiftly laid at Carson's door. 'He gave me some tips for a race I was riding in at Warwick,' she said. 'I won and that really pleased him.'

Fate had thrown them together when she led a horse which Carson was to ride around the paddock. 'I was thrilled when he spoke to me,' she said of their first meeting. 'He was the champion jockey and I was just a stable girl. He always used to speak when I was leading round a horse of his; then one day he turned up at the bungalow I had in Lambourn. I couldn't get over how small he was. It was the first time I'd seen him off a horse and I was used to going out with tall men. But that impression disappeared when we started talking. I was bowled over by his personality and fell in love with him.'

Carson flew home immediately from Hong Kong to try to soften some of the facts. Yes, he had known Suzanne for a year; yes, he had stayed at her parents' house at Kingston; yes, he and Suzanne were good friends. But, when it came to the critical question, he baulked. No, there is no romance. The right answer was soon forthcoming. He moved in with his trainer friend Clive Brittain to try to give himself some breathing space. Although he returned to the family home at Falmouth Cottage, the marriage was effectively over. Carole wore a brave face and insisted that they would remain married, but they were simply words.

Soon Carson had moved in with Suzanne. Carole accepted the inevitable and moved herself and the children out of Falmouth Cottage. Once she had gone, Carson returned to ensconce himself there with Suzanne.

As both Carole and Carson admitted, there was no specific reason for the marriage failing. Yet even granted that inherent danger in all youthful marriages, there are unmistakable signs of the Carson doctrine, that *he* comes before anything, at work.

'I wasn't all that interested in my marriage,' he confessed after it had foundered. 'I was more interested in my career. I don't consider myself a good father either. If the children had come along ten years later, I'd have been a totally different father. The children came when I was young, when I was striving to prove myself. I was more interested in me than them.' He added, and not entirely in jest: 'Nobody should be allowed to marry until they are twenty-five.'

Carson could, perhaps, point to the soundness of his thinking. He had indeed become a hugely successful jockey: a household name, widely liked and admired by the public. But the cost had been high, particularly to the family unit. A marriage over, and the children – Tony, fourteen when it ended, Neil twelve and Ross nine – missing a father's attention. Tony, who works for the Newmarket trainer Willie Jarvis, is reluctant to discuss the subject and becomes sharp and aggressive when it is broached. He confines himself to insisting: 'We get on very well.'

Neil, like his father at one point in his career, works for Clive Brittain. He is less reticent than Tony. 'When he and Mum divorced it was because of his career, nothing else. I've had about five seasons riding on the Flat and over jumps and it's been very hard looking up to him. It has all been a struggle and I haven't had a lot of help. Nowadays I only see him once in a blue moon, and then I'm always being criticised by him. I've done this wrong, done that wrong, I'm in the wrong job. But I was born and bred in racing.'

Ross, the public schoolboy of the family – he went to Radley – and now a conditional jockey, agrees that Carson virtually ignored his children, but is prepared to see mitigating circumstances. 'He was riding six days a week and abroad at weekends. It was the price he had to pay for being successful. I hardly ever see him now. He's always riding and I'm working as well.'

For all Carson's shortcomings as a parent, the children are proud of his achievements. Neil sums up the attitude of all of them: 'You have to admire him because he is still very fit and going so strongly. It is all down to his will to win. You've either got it or you haven't, and there's no question that he's got it. He is very organised with his work, but that was never the case with the family. He

Carson at early-morning exercise
in Hong Kong in 1978

neglected us three children for his riding because he was so determined to get ahead.'

Admiration, respect for his professional achievements, the acknowledgement of a man's determination to triumph, Carson invariably draws the same accolades. Yet after speaking with his children I was forcibly reminded of the chasm separating his public and private personas. There have been times when he would ruthlessly forfeit everything and everyone for the taste of success.

Carson's view of women was perfectly encapsulated by his relationship with Suzanne Kane. He saw them as territories to be conquered and at once subjugated to his way of thinking. He was king in his own domain and his wife or girlfriend was expected to assume unquestioningly the role of subject. Suzanne gave the game away almost immediately. 'The secret of being happy with Willie is to accept that racing is his first love,' she said. 'Any woman must come second.'

In the aftermath of his divorce Carson was free to marry Suzanne had he wished. But he was happy with life as it stood. 'Everything's just great as it is,' he said. 'I don't want things changed.' Suzanne had to toe that line or move on. 'I'd love to get married,' she said, 'but I'd never dream of pushing him into anything. I always let Willie call the tune. He's the boss, a real male chauvinist.'

Carson rushed to agree. He was not going to let slip the opportunity to proclaim to one and all his position as the pre-eminent partner. 'That's just about it,' he said, expounding his superiority with a grin. 'I like a woman in her place. I think she should do what a man says at least eighty per cent of the time.' He did not elaborate on how he believed a woman should behave for the remaining twenty per cent.

Even allowing for Carson's love of playing to the gallery, there is little cause to doubt that he was deadly serious. Suzanne could tell tales of talking to Carson while they were driving to a race meeting. Suddenly he would hit her hard on the thigh and tell her to shut up. 'I didn't mind,' she would say with remarkable good temper. 'It was just his way.' She dreamed about having children but Carson's view was plain enough. 'I've already got three children,' he would say. 'Anyway, she's got horses, what does she want with children?'

One journalist who visited them recalls an interview coming to a close. 'Right,' Carson said, 'ten more minutes then I'm off to the races.' He looked at Suzanne. 'All right,' he barked, 'go and make the tea.' And she did, trotting obediently to the kitchen.

Carson's altered personal circumstances had no ill effects on his professional life. If anything, he was spurred to even greater efforts as he set out to regain his jockeys' title from Pat Eddery.

By the end of the season he was champion again, thanks to a prodigious effort. The *Sporting Life* records that he had 986 rides in 1978 from which he harvested 182 winners. He won by a margin of thirty-four from Eddery, but it is the number of rides which demands attention. Carson drew upon all his application and grim determination to ride anything, anywhere, for anyone. He wanted that title back and he was going to have it. His philosophy was simple: 'If you've got somewhere around a thousand rides in a season then you're going to have winners.'

The arithmetic of the final table proved his argument. Only Sir Gordon Richards, who had precisely 1,000 in 1936, has ever bettered Carson's total of rides. Pat Eddery, himself tireless in his search for winners, had almost 200 fewer mounts than Carson in 1978. It was an outstanding effort by Carson, and it would be a demanding critic indeed who begrudged him his success. If Carson had any complaint about the season it was the lack of top-class winners. Dunfermline and Hot Grove, his two allies from that memorable Jubilee season, remained in training, offering the hope that he would have at least two likely challengers for the big races.

However, neither the Queen nor Lord Leverhulme, the owner of Hot Grove, were to be rewarded for their decisions to keep their horses in training. Dunfermline, particularly, was to prove a disappointment. She ran respectably when second to the French raider Montcontour in the Hardwicke Stakes at Royal Ascot, but was subsequently well beaten in her only two other races. Nor did Carson enjoy much better luck with Hot Grove. He at least did manage one win, in the Westbury Stakes at Sandown, but the fast ground of summer, which did not suit him, hastened his retirement to stud in Newmarket.

But if the older horses were not living up to expectations, Carson did have a couple of two-year-olds, both trained by Hern, who promised great things. More Light, by the Derby winner Morston, had made a spectacular start to his career, winning his first race, at Kempton, by ten lengths. He then stepped up in class to finish a neck second to the highly regarded R. B. Chesne, trained by Henry Cecil, in the Champagne Stakes at Doncaster, and might well have won had he not been hampered in running.

More Light concluded his juvenile career with another second place, this time a rather more conclusive three lengths defeat by the outstanding two-year-old Tromos in the Dewhurst Stakes at Newmarket. He ended the year officially rated 6 lb behind Tromos, and a further 1 lb behind More Light came his stable-companion Troy, a bay colt by Petingo.

After being beaten on his debut at Salisbury, which could be put down largely to inexperience, Troy won a good-class maiden race at Newmarket before moving up in class to take the Champagne Stakes at Goodwood. Hern then opted to rest Troy and bring him back for his final race of the season, the Royal Lodge Stakes at Ascot at the end of September. It was by far his toughest assignment. The unbeaten Lyphards Wish, from Henry Cecil's powerful stable, was the even-money favourite with Troy at 9–4. Ela-Mana-Mou, who had finished second to Troy at Goodwood, was quoted at 10–1, third favourite in the eight-strong field.

'Before the race I thought I'd win,' Carson said. 'My plan was to ride Troy to beat Lyphards Wish, which I did, and then Ela-Mana-Mou came late and did us.' Carson, true to his tactics, had taken the lead from Lyphards Wish inside the final furlong only for Ela-Mana-Mou, produced with a storming late run by Greville Starkey, to grab the spoils from Troy in the dying strides with Lyphards Wish a close third. Time was to show the race had been an excellent test. Each of the first three home would go on to win good races as three-year-olds, but it was Troy and Willie Carson who had gone into many notebooks as the combination to follow.

CHAPTER EIGHT
TROY

Although Carson had now been champion jockey three times, he was still searching for that first Derby winner. The nearest he had come to capturing what Benjamin Disraeli once referred to as 'The Blue Ribbon of the Turf' was when Lester Piggott snatched victory from Carson and Hot Grove in 1977. This would be his eleventh attempt on the great prize in this, its 200th running, and the early indications were heartening. Carson had the proven pair More Light and Troy at his command, and he also had the less experienced but undoubtedly promising Milford to call upon. Milford, owned by the Queen, was bred in the purple, being by the Derby winner Mill Reef out of the Queen's Prix de Diane heroine Highclere.

Owned by Sir Michael Sobell and Sir Arnold Weinstock, Troy represented West Ilsley *par excellence*. The owners of the yard, its incumbent trainer and stable jockey, although from vastly differing backgrounds, were drawn together in a consuming passion for the thoroughbred. Now, in Troy, they had a horse worthy of their combined fervour.

In 1960 Sobell had bought the Ballymacoll Stud in Ireland, and, joined in partnership by his son-in-law, Arnold Weinstock, had succeeded in breeding a steady stream of high-class winners. Weinstock's son, Simon, is not only an integral part of the electronic giant GEC; he is also a racing fanatic, with an encyclopaedic knowledge of the form book and of pedigrees. It was his idea that Milo, a mare by the stayer, Hornbeam, should be mated with the phenomenally fast Petingo. 'If it had been left to me, Troy would never have been produced,' says the now Lord Weinstock. 'I thought £6,000 was a lot of money to pay for a nomination to Petingo.'

Sitting in a pool of light at his desk at GEC headquarters, in London, with paintings of Troy, Ela-Mana-Mou and other family horses adorning the walls, Lord Weinstock was as enthusiastic as a child when talking about his great love, racing. 'I remember one day on the gallops when Troy suddenly stopped and stood still. He was really striking and had such an imperious air. He looked at us as though he was king and we were just dirt.'

The nearest that Sobell and Weinstock had come to winning the Derby was when Scobie Breasley rode Dart Board into third place behind George Moore on Royal Palace in 1967. Hern had gone to Epsom with high hopes of winning the Derby on several occasions since he started training at Newmarket in 1957. In 1962, the subsequent St Leger winner, Hethersett, had been brought down in a pile-up on

Tattenham Hill. The closest the trainer had come to capturing the blue riband had been when Relkino had run the race of his life to take second place behind Empery in 1976.

As usual, the results of the early trials were eagerly awaited. More Light ran well enough when runner-up to Ela-Mana-Mou in the Heath Stakes at Newmarket, but Milford was far more impressive when romping home in the White Rose Stakes at Ascot.

The race chosen for Troy's reappearance was the Classic Trial Stakes, run at Sandown on the same afternoon that the quick-jumping Diamond Edge won the first of his two Whitbread Gold Cups for the legendary Fulke Walwyn. Troy started favourite at 4–7 in a field of five, but it was only in the final stride that Carson finally managed to force his mount past the post a neck in front of Steve Cauthen on Two Of Diamonds.

Lord Weinstock, apart from being the part owner and breeder of the winner, had also taken a further interest in Troy's Derby hopes by backing the colt for himself and his friends at 50–1, after he had been narrowly beaten by Ela-Mana-Mou at Ascot the previous autumn.

On Troy's reappearance he only scrambled home by a neck in the Classic Trial Stakes at Sandown. 'Troy wasn't impressive. It was very, very wet. Steve took Two Of Diamonds right over on to the far rails whereas Willie brought Troy very wide on the outside.'

Now the guessing game about Carson's likely mount began in earnest. Lord Weinstock, with a businessman's logical mind, thoroughly disapproved of the whole process, considering it unfair to the respective owners. One morning at breakfast at West Ilsley, the tycoon, his patience thinning by the day, glared at Carson. 'You'd better make up your mind,' he said. Willie demurred and Hern leapt to the defence of his contract rider. 'Willie's got the right to make up his mind when he's ready to do so.' 'I still think it's an unsatisfactory state of affairs,' said Weinstock, still unhappy, but bending sufficiently to give Carson more time. The decision-making took place within the confines of Willie's careful thought processes and also in the secret world of the West Ilsley gallops.

Milford, a freer mover than Troy, was the better worker of the pair at home, but Carson was not deceived. Brian Procter, chief work rider at West Ilsley, knows Willie well and trusts his judgement implicitly. 'He's been a first-class picker of the right horse over the years. He's got a very logical approach. He weighs things up very carefully and never rushes into anything. He just keeps plodding away and racking his brain a bit.'

The jockey's ideas were only going one way, however. 'Normally you have to try and read between the lines with Willie,' Procter went on, 'but not on this occasion. One day we galloped the two horses together over a mile and a half. Willie rode Troy and I was on Milford. When we were pulling up, he suddenly said excitedly, "This is the one, Brian, this is the one." ' The reason for Carson's enthusiasm became apparent to Procter about a week later. 'I was lucky enough to get a ride on Troy. I gave him a smack round the shoulder and suddenly found out what it was all about. He was a very laid-back horse behind the bridle. But when you got into him, he'd really accelerate for you.'

Willie nearly missed riding Troy, not only in his next intended race, the Predominate Stakes at Goodwood, but also in the Derby. At Chester on 10 May the jockey was riding Lidgate for Harry Wragg in the last race. After attempting to make all the running, the 11–10 favourite had been headed when he suddenly crashed to the ground. Hern was watching from the stands. 'I'm afraid my point of view was very selfish,' the trainer remembers. 'When I saw Willie flying through the air, the thought immediately flashed into my mind, "Who on earth am I going to get to ride Troy in the Derby?" '

A hospital examination revealed that the jockey had fractured his right collar-bone and torn some knee ligaments. He decided to discharge himself the next morning and went to the races, but was obviously in great pain.

With Willie sidelined, Joe Mercer took over on Milford the following Saturday and the Queen's colt remained a live contender for the Derby when romping home by an easy seven lengths in the Lingfield Derby Trial. But at York the following week, More Light virtually put himself out of Classic contention when, with Pat Eddery in the saddle, the colt could finish only fourth to Lyphards Wish in the Mecca-Dante Stakes.

Decision day for Carson arrived on 23 May. The press descended on Goodwood, where Willie, having his first mount since his accident, finished third on Roehampton in the opening Tegleaze Stakes. Without a shadow of a doubt, Troy was highly impressive when beating Serge Lifar by seven lengths in the Predominate Stakes. He looked magnificent in the paddock and had tightened up since Sandown, although his trainer had clearly left something to work on before Derby day. Although the opposition was of no particular account, the colt had won without coming off the bridle. Troy had also shown that he possessed a calm and relaxed temperament and the only question now remaining was that of his ultimate ability.

Carson refused to make a statement, saying rather pompously that he needed the evening to think the matter over. Not so the media, and when Willie appeared on the Goodwood balcony the next day to announce that he was riding Troy, the jockey's decision had already been anticipated in the headlines in that morning's newspapers. Lester Piggott, already with eight Derbys to his credit, was booked for the discarded Milford. Niniski, the third stable runner, was ridden by John Reid.

Derby day started badly for Willie as he finished unplaced in the first two races. But the jockey was still full of confidence when, wearing the light blue colours with the yellow cap, he took Troy through the long preliminaries and then up the hill on the way to the start. Ela-Mana-Mou was 9–2 favourite with Troy next at 6–1. Milford followed at 15–2.

Lyphards Wish was the first to show, setting a steady, level pace which Troy

The first Derby win:
Troy comes home seven lengths clear of Dickens Hill
in the 1979 Epsom Derby, the 200th running of the race

struggled to keep up with. Lyphards Wish still showed the way round Tattenham Corner with Milford in second and Troy, on the inside rail, no better than mid-division in the field of twenty-three. With two and a half furlongs remaining Lyphards Wish was making the best of his way home, but Carson had by now begun to extricate Troy from his potential prison on the inside. When Carson had worked Troy across to the outside, the race was turned on its head. With Carson asking Troy for his effort, the colt accelerated as though jet-propelled. Two furlongs out, Troy still had at least half-a-dozen horses in front of him, but before he had reached the final furlong he was in front and powering further clear with every stride. At the line he had seven lengths in hand of the Irish challenger Dickens Hill, the greatest winning margin since Manna in 1925.

This bald description presents a vivid contrast to the conflicting emotions felt by those involved. Lord Weinstock for example: 'Coming down the hill he was going backwards and I thought that there was something wrong as he was running two stone below his form. Then when they came into the straight and pulled off the rails I thought he might finish fourth. He went like a rocket and did the last two furlongs in the equivalent time of fifty-five seconds for five furlongs. It was an amazing performance.'

Carson's view: 'Turning into Tattenham Corner, my fella started to grab the

LEFT *Willie clowning after Troy's Derby win*

OPPOSITE *Winning the King George VI and Queen Elizabeth Stakes on Troy, from Gay Mecene (right), at Ascot in 1979*

ground, like he'd six-inch nails in his feet. Ahead of me I could see everything slowing up. They had gone too fast and were coming back. That's where English jockeys don't get any credit even though I'd got it right. They think that Americans and Australians are the only ones with clocks in their heads.'

There is no doubt that Willie had shown tremendous courage in sitting and suffering for so long before achieving one of his life's ambitions. If he had panicked at the top of the hill and started to get at Troy too early he could have sickened the horse in a few strides. 'Troy was a good stayer, he was strong and athletic,' Carson said. 'But he didn't have a turn of foot, he didn't quicken, he just lengthened. In the Derby they went very, very fast and I had the confidence to sit and suffer. But suddenly the pace is very fast and I am going nowhere. Coming down the hill I thought, "Well, it's not this year either, another disappointment".'

For some reason, Troy's Derby form has always had its detractors. Indeed, to this day, the official handicappers swear that Troy was the only horse in the field

capable of staying a mile and a half at racing pace. But as the runner-up, Dickens Hill went on to win the Eclipse, and Northern Baby the third horse home, the Champion Stakes and Ela-Mana-Mou next time out won the mile and a half King Edward VII Stakes at Ascot, their reasoning defies comprehension.

The next day, racing at Epsom was abandoned after a thunderstorm. So a proud and happy Dick Hern climbed the endless steps leading to the press room at the top of the grandstand. The Major laughed and joked as he drank champagne, celebrating the fact that he had at last won the Derby after so many disappointments.

The long-term plan was the Prix de l'Arc de Triomphe, a race that the Weinstocks coveted above all others. More immediately, the intention was to go to the Curragh for the Irish Derby. Once again Troy beat Dickens Hill, although this time the deficit was reduced to four lengths. And then came the King George VI and Queen Elizabeth Diamond Stakes, in which Troy met the older horses for the first time. And, as often happens on these occasions, Troy put up a workmanlike, rather than brilliant, performance, when beating the French four-year-old Gay Mecene by one and a half lengths with his old rival, Ela-Mana-Mou, finishing three lengths away third.

In August, there came a surprise decision when Troy was brought back to a mile and a quarter. Although the dual Derby winner had to work hard over this shorter distance to beat Crimson Beau by three-quarters of a length, this hard-earned victory represented a magnificent feat of training by Hern, who was as happy and proud after the race as I have ever seen him.

Troy's York win had lifted his first prize money earnings to £415,738, a record for a European-trained colt at that time, which had only been surpassed by the fillies Dahlia and Allez France. Unfortunately, Troy had had a hard race, and Lord Weinstock for one did not appreciate it. 'Both Willie and Dick had wanted to run, but I had been dead against it. To bring him back to a mile and a quarter was all wrong. He should have gone for one of the Arc trial races like the Niel. It's a big disadvantage to go to Longchamp for the first time.'

The idiosyncratic and independent-minded owner also considered that Carson made a rare misjudgement when Troy met his only defeat in finishing third to Three Troikas in the Arc. 'Willie rode a bad race. He dropped the horse out coming down the hill and finished up on the outside of the field where the ground was worst. Then he went too soon and finished well beaten.'

I believe Lord Weinstock is being less than fair to his rider. Carson appeared to give the horse every chance, judged by the way he had been ridden in his previous races. But there is no doubt that in finishing three lengths and one length behind Three Troikas and Le Marmot the colt had run well below his best. There are so many imponderables in assessing a sub-standard performance. The ground, for example, was softer at Longchamp than Troy, a good actioned but heavy horse, was likely to enjoy. The English Classic programme always seems to take a great deal out of a horse. A great many other reputations have foundered in Paris on the first Sunday in October. It is worth remembering that Mill Reef and Dancing Brave are still the only British horses to have won or run well in the 2,000 Guineas, Derby and King George and gone on to triumph in the Arc as three-year-olds.

While Lord Weinstock was left to wonder whether the hard race at York had cost his colt the Arc, Carson reflected on Troy's accomplishments that season. 'He's the best I've ridden,' he said. 'He did more than most Derby winners. They said that by the time of the Arc he'd had a hard season, but it was the ground. He was such a big, heavy horse he couldn't handle it. I suppose you could argue he wasn't a true champion because he couldn't handle the going, but to me he was still a great horse.'

For all his big-race glory, Carson was forced to relinquish his jockeys' title to Joe Mercer by 164 winners to 142. It was a neat irony: Carson had supplanted Mercer at West Ilsley but Mercer, now riding as stable jockey to the powerful Henry Cecil string, had at least taken a measure of revenge. But for Carson this was the year when he at last made his mark in the Derby; when he joined the roll of the many great jockeys who had won the blue riband. This had been the year of Troy.

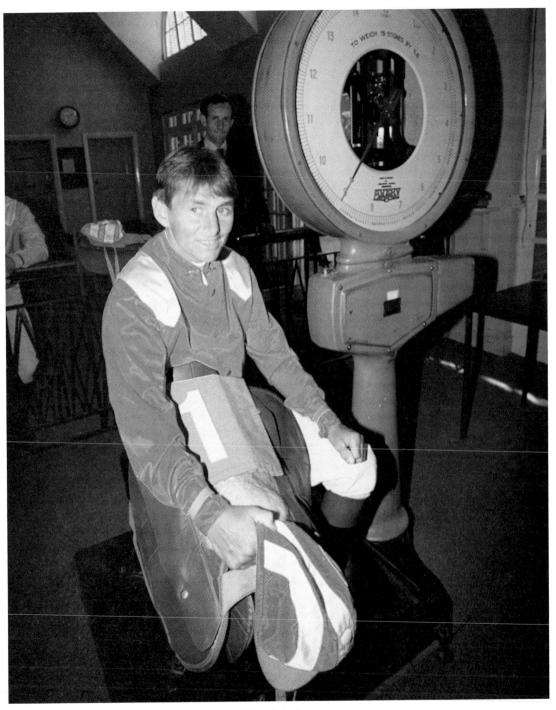

All weighed up:
Carson goes to scale at Newmarket in 1979. He has always had
the great advantage of being able to ride at 7st 12lb

CHAPTER NINE

FIVE CLASSICS

Troy's Derby win in 1979 represented one of the towering peaks of Carson's career. But by the end of 1980 he bestrode the Classic scene like some five-foot colossus. During the campaign he rode five Classic winners and was champion jockey for the fourth time with a total of 166 winners. It was an extraordinary season, as so much of the jockey's success had been impossible to predict. Three of his Classic victories, those of Henbit in the Derby, Bireme in the Oaks and Shoot A Line in the Irish Oaks were gained on horses trained by Hern.

Yet, in the middle of April, just over six weeks before Epsom, the trainer had driven away from the Craven meeting at Newmarket having failed to register a solitary three-year-old success. 'I'm afraid we haven't got much this year,' he observed gloomily to his wife Sheilah. West Ilsley's only winner at the meeting had come when Willie had driven Ela-Mana-Mou to a hard-earned victory over Haul Knight and Cracaval in the Earl of Sefton Stakes. However, the colt turned out to be one of the largest contributors to Hern's third trainer's title, with record British earnings of £831,964.

A former rival of Troy, Ela-Mana-Mou had been trained by Guy Harwood as a three-year-old. Bought for the modest outlay of 4,500 guineas as a yearling, on behalf of Mrs Andry Muinos, who also had the good fortune to own the 1981 2,000 Guineas winner To-Agori-Mou, the colt was sold to Tim Rogers, of Airlie Stud in Ireland and the Weinstock family for half a million pounds prior to the 1980 season. After winning four races in succession for his new connections, including the Eclipse Stakes and the King George VI, Ela-Mana-Mou was then beaten only about half a length when third to Detroit in the Arc. He was syndicated to stand as a stallion in Ireland, with a capital value of £3.2 million.

The Classic picture, as far as the colts were concerned, was dominated by Nureyev, bought as a yearling in Keeneland, Kentucky, after a sensational bidding duel between Stavros Niarchos's representatives and Robert Sangster. Niarchos won the day and the Northern Dancer colt was first sent to be trained by Peter Walwyn at Lambourn but was transferred to François Boutin before he ran.

So impressive had Nureyev been when winning his only start as a two-year-old, and again while cantering home by six lengths on his seasonal reappearance in the

Prix Djebel at Maisons-Laffitte, that the French challenger started a heavily backed 13–8 favourite for the 2,000 Guineas.

The race was one of the most dramatic ever seen, and the controversial issues highlighted that afternoon are still a matter of debate. To put it simply, Philippe Paquet rode Nureyev with total disregard for the opposition. Dropping the favourite out so far behind that they were over ten lengths adrift at half-way, the jockey found himself trapped behind a wall of horses. Barging his way through, and in the process knocking Pat Eddery and Posse for six, Nureyev took up the running and resisted the attacks of Carson on Known Fact, trained by Jeremy Tree, and also of Posse, to win by a neck and three-quarters of a length. Disqualification was inevitable, and

Carson and Ela-Mana-Mou before winning
the Earl of Sefton Stakes at Newmarket in 1980

Carson, previously successful on High Top in 1972, was handed his second Guineas virtually on a plate.

Carson was doubly fortunate, for if Posse had not been hampered the Dunlop-trained colt would undoubtedly have finished second and might well have beaten Nureyev. After the disqualification had been announced, the dejected connections of Nureyev, together with the media, trooped into the stewards' room to watch the camera patrol film. A vivid imprint remains of an angry but still proud Boutin arguing the toss with the authorities as the horror movie progressed. Niarchos, the diminutive Greek shipping tycoon, stood with his arms folded, viewing the film dispassionately.

Critics of the Jockey Club's Rule 153, which deals with interference during races, had a field day. In this instance, Nureyev was placed last so that Paquet could be found guilty of reckless riding and suspended for seven days. They argued that the British rule, which insists that the jockey and the horse are considered as one unit in these circumstances, is basically unfair to the connections of the horse. They much preferred the French rule which allows more flexibility to the stewards. For example, if the Guineas had been run at Longchamp, Paquet could have been punished, but Nureyev could have been placed third behind Posse, the horse he hampered. No one could have argued with this.

The first of the Hern dark horses for the Derby to come on view was Henbit, who, like Troy the year before, was aimed at the Classic Trial at Sandown. Bought for $24,000 as a yearling on behalf of Mrs Arpad Plesch, who had already won a Derby with Psidium, Henbit was in due course to become the seventh American-bred winner of the Derby in the past twelve years.

A generous 33–1 was available about Henbit for the Derby after the colt had just got the better of Huguenot, Ginistrelli and Master Willie, but only because the winner was at first thought to be going for the French Derby instead. The pace of the Derby build-up started to increase. A telephone call to Hern on the Sunday morning, the day after the Sandown race, produced a guarded response. 'Henbit is very well and runs in the Chester Vase.' Coded messages like this were disregarded at the recipient's peril. Hern, an old-fashioned trainer who considered his business to be his owners' and not that of the press, was never more forthcoming than this.

The sharp circuit of the Roodeye at Chester proved no problem for the improving Henbit. Acting smoothly round the bends like the proverbial top, the even-money favourite beat Moomba Masquerade by four lengths. Ridden along in front on the final circuit, the colt took some time to find his stride. But Henbit had proved almost beyond doubt his ability to handle Epsom. So the plan to go to Chantilly for the Prix du Jockey-Club was scrapped, and the colt became a strong fancy for the Derby.

The next afternoon, Carson was on even better terms with himself after Shoot A Line had stormed home by five lengths to beat Little Bonny in the Cheshire Oaks. Although the filly had been ill at ease round the bends she was clearly a high-class stayer in embryo.

The word had been abroad for some time that West Ilsley housed an exceptional

At Tattenham Corner in the 1980 Derby. Henbit (spotted colours)
is perfectly positioned just behind the leaders

crop of prospective middle-distance fillies. And at York the week after Chester, Bireme made a deep impression when beating the Lingfield Oaks Trial winner, Gift Wrapped, in the Musidora Stakes. Informed opinion was that Carson would choose to ride the York winner at Epsom, despite the ease of Shoot A Line's win at Chester. Nor was this view disturbed at Newbury the following Friday after Sir John Astor's one-eyed filly, The Dancer, had stormed home by seven lengths in the Sir Charles Clore Memorial Stakes.

In the following afternoon's Mecca-Dante Stakes, Carson rode Water Mill. A possible rival to Henbit for his services at Epsom, the Mill Reef colt had been slow to come to hand and was considered to be in need of the race when finishing third to Hello Gorgeous. In the circumstances, Water Mill had run a satisfactory Derby trial, but after due reflection Willie chose to ride Henbit. Tony Murray was booked not only for Water Mill but also for Shoot A Line in the Oaks. Ernie Johnson was asked to ride The Dancer in the fillies' Classic.

On the day, a run on Nikoli saw the Irish 2,000 Guineas winner start favourite at 4–1. Henbit was second choice in the market at 7–1, followed by Lester Piggott's mount, the hitherto disappointing Monteverdi at 8–1. Hello Gorgeous, the Dante winner, and Tyrnavos were both 9–1 chances. The race itself was as competitive as the betting suggested. Henbit was never going particularly well and Carson was pumping and pushing virtually throughout. Two furlongs from home at least nine horses were still in with a chance. Pulling Henbit off the fence, Willie drove the colt into the lead past Rankin. Soon after that, Henbit faltered to his right, but straightened out and hung on gamely to his lead to beat Master Willie by three-quarters of a length. It had been a heroic performance by the winner as he finished virtually on three legs after cracking an off fore cannon bone. The accident had presumably occurred when the colt had hung to the right approaching the last furlong.

Carson had excelled himself on the crippled winner. Never had his astute tactical brain worked to better advantage than in the way he managed to keep Henbit up with the gallop throughout. Never has his strength been more evident than in that desperate final furlong. Years later, Pat Eddery still pays tribute to Carson's perseverance. 'Willie pinched the Derby on Henbit. He almost certainly wasn't that good a horse. Willie rode a perfect race and got a Derby winner out of a not really star colt.'

Carson was deeply impressed and moved by Henbit's courage. 'He was a really game horse. He broke a bone and still won it. But all I felt was that he'd changed legs. The adrenalin was pumping and I didn't realise he had gone lame. Of course you can see it watching the film.' Henbit was patched up and brought back into training for two modest runs as a four-year-old, after which he was retired to stud in Ireland.

What an astonishing year it was for setbacks to top-class horses. Apart from Henbit, Nureyev contracted a viral chill and was never seen in public again. And Bireme, on whom Willie gained a decisive win over Vielle and The Dancer in the Oaks on the Saturday after the Derby, injured herself when getting loose on the roads, soon after her Epsom win. Bireme, also, never ran again.

The Sunday after the Oaks, Willie's unforgettable year continued when he rode Policeman to a shock win in the Prix du Jockey-Club, at 54–1. The reasons for Policeman's improved form were two-fold. He was tackling a mile and a half for the first time, and it was also the first occasion that the colt had met the redoubtable and dynamic Carson, who was in such irresistible form. Having pressed on from half-way and then 'waited for the others to attack', the assault Carson expected never arrived. The enterprisingly ridden Policeman kept going to beat Shakapour by one and a half lengths.

A comic aftermath of this win was that a crate of champagne arrived in the weighing room. Carson cheerfully dispensed the welcome drink to his fellow jockeys, but his amusement turned to disgust when he realised it was not a gift and he was presented with an exorbitant bill.

Seldom have there ever been so many talented fillies in training as there were in

Bireme wins the 1980 Oaks for Willie

1980. Shoot A Line ran well below her best at Epsom, looking unhappy beforehand and running indifferently before finishing a remote fifth, but after that Shoot A Line was undefeated, her four further victories including impressive wins in the Irish and Yorkshire Oaks.

At Ascot, in the King George, Carson was inspired on Ela-Mana-Mou when recording the second of his four wins in Britain's most important all-aged race. By

now the jockey's three wins on the Weinstocks' battling four-year-old had taught the jockey exactly how to use the colt's stamina and fighting qualities to best advantage. Suddenly opening up a clear lead approaching the straight, Ela-Mana-Mou left most of the opposition floundering. Then came the ultimate confrontation between Carson on the eventual winner and the jockey's old rival Lester Piggott on Mrs Penny. The famous posterior was high in the air as the 'long fellow' was confidently waiting to pounce on what appeared to be his struggling rival. But having used Ela-Mana-Mou's pugnacity to compensate for the colt's lack of finishing pace,

Carson had blunted Mrs Penny's speed. After a finish reminiscent of the epic battle between Grundy and Bustino five years earlier the colt held on to beat the filly by three-quarters of a length.

What a magnificent feat of training did the whole of Ela-Mana-Mou's third season career represent by Hern, to improve the colt 7 lb on the form he had shown from Pulborough. And privately Carson had expressed fears that it was unlikely to prove a bargain buy.

'Guy Harwood's lot thought they had come out of it well,' remembers Ted Eley. 'Willie said it was a waste of time and that he was gone in the shoulders. He didn't

OPPOSITE *Ela-Mana-Mou wins the King George VI and Queen Elizabeth Diamond Stakes at Ascot in Carson's glorious year of 1980*

LEFT *Carson with Joe Mercer, the man he replaced at West Ilsley, after Mercer had been awarded the OBE in 1980*

come down the hill racing into the dip when winning at Newmarket so they kept him on level or uphill courses after that.' Lord Weinstock also remembers. 'An American vet thought there was something wrong with his back. But Dick found someone to treat it, who'd been treating him at Harwood's. Willie got on with the horse and Dick understood him, so between them they knew exactly what to do.'

The jockey rode so many magnificent races during that golden year, and at Ascot in September there was a tremendous set-to between Kris and Known Fact in the Queen Elizabeth II Stakes. It was an epic contest. Kris, having won fifteen of his

Willie (left) edges out his longtime rival
Lester Piggott at Sandown in 1980

sixteen races in three seasons, was being compared to Brigadier Gerard as one of the outstanding milers of all time. But Known Fact, reflecting the highest credit on Jeremy Tree, looked in tremendous shape and may have improved 5 lb since being awarded the 2,000 Guineas in the spring. After a thrilling tussle, Known Fact wore down Kris to win by a neck, the pair finishing six lengths clear of Gift Wrapped.

In Paris on 6 October, Willie once again excelled himself on Ela-Mana-Mou as the pair attempted to give the Weinstocks that longed-for first triumph in the Arc.

The ground was firm, so Hern had fitted felt pads between the soles of the colt's feet and his racing plates. The cheering from the thousands of British visitors rose in a crescendo as the gallant pair burst into the lead early in the straight. They looked uncatchable, but in the last furlong Pat Eddery and Detroit came storming up on the outside to overhaul the colt a hundred yards from home. Argument also came home strongly to finish second, a short head in front of Ela-Mana-Mou and half a length behind the winner.

For Lord Weinstock, still without a win in the Arc, the memory hurts. 'Detroit was pouring with sweat from two and a half furlongs out and Pat gave her a real pounding. Somehow I thought it was impossible for her to win, but he conjured it out of her. They came through on the wide outside and Ela-Mana-Mou didn't have time to fight back.'

Carson and Known Fact (No. 5) narrowly get the better of Joe Mercer
and Kris in a stirring battle
for the Queen Elizabeth II Stakes at Ascot in 1980

CHAPTER TEN
'LUCKY TO BE ALIVE'

Any time a jockey comes off a horse, the newspapers, particularly the more garish tabloids, reach for their tried and trusted headlines. 'Jockey narrowly escapes death', 'Lucky to be alive', 'How I survived' scream at us from the front and back pages. Exactly how great the danger is, of course, beside the point.

But at York's August meeting in 1981 those headlines meant exactly what they said. Willie Carson did indeed narrowly escape death; he was lucky to be alive. In the Yorkshire Oaks, one of the season's most important races for fillies, Carson rode the 16–1 outsider Silken Knot, trained by Dick Hern. Carson, employing his preferred tactics of keeping his mount close to the leaders, was lying third as the field turned into York's long, sweeping straight. As they straightened up for the dash for home, Silken Knot's forelegs broke without warning, catapulting Carson into the ground. The horses following were unable to avoid him and galloped over him as he lay on the turf.

In the silence as the field moved away, Carson lay motionless, a crumpled heap. The stricken Silken Knot attempted to struggle to her feet, but collapsed again. She had to be destroyed. It was an awful moment. The fall had been watched not only by a huge crowd at the track but by millions more on television. Steve Cauthen, who, on Viendra, had been one of those desperately trying to avoid Carson, described the fall as 'the worst I have ever seen'.

Carson, unconscious and bleeding from the ears, was lifted gently into the racecourse ambulance. The ambulance picked its way gingerly up the course, a certain sign of possible serious injury for its passenger, before going straight to York District Hospital. The wait for news was agonising. Anyone who saw the fall knew its severity. When the news came, it was almost a relief. Carson had a fractured skull, a broken left wrist and a fractured vertebra. Serious injuries, certainly, but mercifully he would live to fight another day.

Dr Michael Allen, the medical consultant to the Jockey Club, imposed the mandatory three-month riding ban on Carson. The ban is immediately applied in the case of head injuries, to prevent jockeys taking the question of recuperation into their own hands and returning before it is safe for them to do so. After visiting him the day after the accident, Dr Allen delivered the verdict that the jockey's admirers had been waiting to hear. 'My opinion is that he will be well and fit enough to ride next season,' he said. 'He is in good spirits but beginning to realise just how lucky he was. He is thankful to be in one piece.'

Although battered and bruised, Carson was discharged a week later. His spell at the hospital had transformed its quiet into something between a branch office of Interflora, as well-wishers swamped his room with flowers and get well cards, and a vaudeville show, as Carson insisted on touring the wards to cheer up other patients. 'I didn't learn much more about nursing while he was here,' one of the nurses observed, 'but I picked up a hell of a lot about flower arranging.'

The reaction to Carson's fall says plenty about the affection in which he is held

*Willie lies motionless after his dreadful fall
from the stricken Silken Knot at York in 1981*

by the public. Principal among the enquirers after his well-being was the Queen, who made a point of telephoning Carson's mother, May, to ask to be kept informed of his progress. Many thousands more went to the time, trouble and expense of writing him letters and cards, and sending presents.

As Carson began his convalescence he had plenty of time to reflect upon the fall. 'Silken Knot had been a disappointing filly but she'd always worked well at home. We tried her in blinkers and she beat some good fillies on the gallops, so I went

Carson perking up in hospital after his fall,
thanks to the attention of two nurses

to York feeling confident. I thought I would win; the blinkers had transformed her. But I suppose she must have been saving a weakness somehow. During the race the legs just snapped, crack, crack, like a couple of gunshots. That was it. People often don't realise how badly Flat jockeys can suffer in a fall. Although the jump boys have a hundred per cent higher risk of getting hurt, they have slower falls and they expect them. When it happens to us it comes harder and faster. Then it can be very serious.'

The darkest days were the two weeks which followed his release from hospital. Unable to move without assistance, his spirits plummeted. 'Those first ten days at home were terrible,' he was to recall. 'I think that all the pills they had given me were driving me mad. There were times when I wondered if I was finished, if it was all over. If there had been a gun at the side of the bed I think I would have shot myself. Then I decided to get rid of all the pills, and I started improving the very next day.' Once he had come to terms with the injuries, there was another, perhaps even tougher, obstacle to surmount: the three-month lay-off. For someone of Carson's inherent energy and barely suppressed desire always to get on with the job, the days of inactivity were hard to bear. 'It had a terrible effect on me mentally,' he remembers. 'When the incentive to hurry back was gone I just had to sit and suffer. I understand why the doctor put the ban on me, and I know that he was doing it in my own best interests, but it really didn't help. It took away the need to fight the pain, and perhaps that would have helped me more.'

Carson's state of mind was not helped by the knowledge that he had been ten winners clear of Lester Piggott in the quest for a fourth jockeys' title. With Carson out of action, the way was clear for Piggott to take the championship as he pleased. He did so with the greatest of ease, amassing 179 winners by the end of the season. Astonishingly, Carson, despite missing some three months of the season, still held on to second place with 114 successes. Carson's claim that 'Lester would have been a very tired man by the end of the season if I'd still been around' was beyond argument. But Carson had survived a dangerous fall, was in trim for the new season and, most threatening of all for his rivals, was coming back with a score to settle.

The question every jockey must answer when he returns from a fall is whether his nerve will hold. Does he still have the resolution to be in the thick of the fight?; will he force his mount towards that narrow gap in front of him?; or will he pull back and wait for an easier, less risky, opportunity to make ground? Willie Carson was no different. He returned to the saddle for the opening of the 1982 season determined to regain his jockeys' title from Piggott. His abilities and his expertise, honed over the years, remained as sharp as ever, but had his will to win survived that savage fall?

Carson is no great lover of Doncaster in March. 'It gives me that Monday morning feeling,' was his succinct view of the meeting where the Flat season slips almost apologetically into action. He began with four rides, and although a winner eluded him he collected a second in the day's most valuable race. He had, more significantly, shown that he had put his fall behind him. The next day he collected his first winner, Cheka, in the Doncaster Town Plate, and his challenge to regain the title had begun in earnest.

As we watched him climb back into top gear, the thought occurred that perhaps we had underestimated his raw spirit, the almost primitive desire that had borne him from the back streets of Stirling all those years ago. Nothing had stopped him before, and no fall was going to stand in his way now. If there were any after effects, Carson kept them well concealed.

Carson has always insisted that the fall, while physically horrendous, had never touched him mentally. 'It has never affected me because I can't remember a thing

*Elaine and Willie after their register office wedding
in Chester in May 1982*

about it. Of course, people have told me how bad the fall was, but for me it's as though it never happened. I can block it out completely.

'I've only once been affected by a fall and that was at Chester in 1979. I was riding a horse called Lidgate for Harry Wragg in a seven-furlong race. We were in that very short straight there and all of a sudden the horse just dropped. There was absolutely no reason for it. Then it just picked itself up and galloped off. That frightened me, that it happened without any obvious cause. I wouldn't have been bothered if it had slipped, or hit the heels of another horse. Then I would have known why. It was months before I could get that out of my mind, that a horse could just go down and there would be no explanation. Apart from anything else I broke a collar-bone.'

Now Carson has rather happier memories of the Chester May meeting. On 5 May 1982 he married Elaine Williams at Chester Register Office before dashing to the course for five rides. One of them, Swiftfoot, showed a suitable sense of occasion by winning the Cheshire Oaks. Elaine and her parents returned to the family home, Haughton Hall Farm, to watch him ride on television. 'The honeymoon will have to wait until the end of the season,' she said. 'For now the best wedding present is to have a winner.'

Carson met Elaine at a jockeys' dinner in York in the months after Suzanne Kane had left his life. Elaine had gone with an old friend and ended up sitting next to Carson. She was twenty-five, a country girl; the daughter of John and Betty Williams, farmers from Cheshire. Willie was a confirmed hunting fan. He rode with the famous Quorn Hunt and then with the Cheshire. He told Elaine that he was due to visit Cheshire the following day to hunt and then attend a dinner. Would she like to join him? She accepted, but doubted that she would ever hear from him. But Carson did telephone, did take her to dinner and, as she says, 'it developed from there'.

After his fall at York she had been the first by his bedside with an armful of flowers, and had helped him through the long months of recovery. She had also played acting secretary as Carson ploughed through the 5,000 letters and cards he had received from well-wishers. Like Carole and Suzanne before her, Elaine was to give up her own life to help Carson pursue his own excellence. At first she organised his rides, but eventually found that she was 'just not cut out for that.' After their marriage, she also gave up her own catering business. 'Once racing starts, life is terribly hectic,' she says. 'I'm chief cook and bottle-washer, the gardener and the secretary.'

Willie has nothing but praise for her loyalty. 'Elaine has been very supportive to me,' he says. 'She has been dedicated to me and my style of life.' Dedication to Carson and his lifestyle is the recurring theme of his women. In the early days Carole had worked day and night to keep the family together, book his rides and make sure the road was clear for Carson's march to the top; Suzanne had accepted that she could never be number one in Carson's life, only second best to racing; now Elaine trod the same path. Clearly Carson has inspired such loyalty in his wives and girlfriends that they have gladly played second fiddle to his profession. Yet there

Elaine and Willie at a Derby Day dinner

is an inescapable feeling that the signing away of independence was never negotiable; it is a basic demand of Carson's that nothing, no marriage, no relationship, can be allowed to hinder his professional ambitions.

Appropriately, Swiftfoot, the wedding day winner, was to prove one of Carson's most productive mounts of the season. Although she finished last of thirteen in the Oaks, she returned to her best form to win the Irish Oaks at the Curragh and the valuable Park Hill Stakes at Doncaster's St Leger meeting. She also finished second in the Yorkshire Oaks, narrowly failing to give Carson what would have been a famous victory in the race in which he suffered serious injuries just a year earlier.

Yet Carson's season was to become more famous for a defeat than for any of his 145 winners, and second place to Piggott, that year. An hour after Swiftfoot's narrow defeat in the Yorkshire Oaks, Carson teamed up with Gorytus, a marvellously attractive son of Nijinsky, in the Acomb Stakes. Their seven lengths victory from the previously unbeaten Salieri was the stuff of Classic dreams. Bookmakers were inundated as backers struggled to secure the best prices for next season's 2,000 Guineas and Derby. The Knavesmire buzzed with the belief that we could truly have seen a great horse that afternoon.

That impression was confirmed when Gorytus was an easy winner of the Champagne Stakes at Doncaster. His next, and final, appearance that season, the Dewhurst Stakes at Newmarket, was viewed by all as little more than a formality. In a field of four he was the 1–2 favourite, with Diesis, the winner of the Middle Park Stakes at Newmarket, another of the season's top two-year-old tests, considered his only serious rival at 2–1. Gordian and Tough Commander, who completed the line-up, were unfancied at 33–1 and 200–1 respectively.

The race was a sensation. Carson restrained Gorytus towards the rear of the field, apparently travelling well. But at about half-way in the seven-furlong race, Gorytus began to look distressed. He started to lose touch with the other three runners, who gradually left him behind. He fell further and further behind until he was completely detached and all but pulled up in last place. One commentator offered the perfect observation: 'Carson keeps looking down at Gorytus's legs as though a wheel has fallen off,' he said.

It was as though the clock had stopped. Trainers, jockeys, spectators, anyone, in fact, who had witnessed the race, wrestled to digest the sight before them. As Gorytus straggled home the air was thick with suspicion. Had he been nobbled? Carson's immediate reaction fuelled the thought. 'It's just as though he'd been got at,' he said. 'Gorytus ran like a dead horse.' Mrs Peter Walwyn, the wife of the trainer, caught the mood. 'That was a horrible thing to happen,' she said. 'It's bad for racing, it's bad for everyone.'

After Gorytus had been led away from the unsaddling enclosure I went to see him in the racecourse stables. He stood tired and dejected, like an unfit man who had

Gorytus going to post for the sensational Dewhurst Stakes at Newmarket, October 1980. Gorytus finished last to Diesis in a blaze of rumour and speculation

been forced to run for miles. Barely a quarter of an hour earlier he had been full of vigour in the paddock and had moved to the post with a glorious freedom.

'He stood solid as a rock when I saddled him,' Hern remembers. 'Just as good as gold. When he came back after the race his heartbeat was incredibly high, although it had returned to normal by the time we took him to the stables.'

Hern is as mystified now as he was then. Immediately after the race Hern and Carson were interviewed in the inevitable stewards' enquiry. The stewards issued a statement: 'Major Hern was unable to account for the poor performance of the colt, and stated that Gorytus had been blood tested on Monday and Wednesday with perfect results [the race was run on Friday]. The colt had also eaten up on the previous evening and on the morning of the race. The colt pulled up extremely distressed after the race and this was confirmed by the racecourse vet. Carson added that Gorytus was unable to produce anything when asked to go on three furlongs out.' The mystery continued to intrigue racing in the days and weeks which followed. By the next day Gorytus had returned to normal in his box at West Ilsley, but when I pressed Hern on his mood before the race he answered: 'Of course I was worried. How could I fail to be when other horses in the yard were coughing?'

At the time Hern had not made public that there was coughing in the stable. Hern's aim had certainly not been deliberately to mislead people, but, as a trainer of the old school, his views have always been based on the tenet that his horses' well-being is the business of the owners, not of the general public.

Feelings ran high in the aftermath of the race, and Hern was by no means immune from criticism. 'Everyone knew that Gorytus was wrong except Dick Hern,' ran one common stricture. 'Why did he run him?' Granted it might have been prudent for Hern to have warned the public about the coughing at West Ilsley, but I believe the criticism to have been unfair. Hern sent Gorytus to Newmarket in the belief that the colt was fit and ready to run for his life. The trainer stood by his actions then, and even now, some ten years later, is convinced he did the right thing. The coughing, he maintains, could not account for such a dismal showing by a potentially top-class colt.

Assuming Hern to be right, that leaves a far more unpalatable alternative: foul play. Was it dope that made Gorytus fail so dismally? That cannot be answered any more definitively now than at the time of the race. The tests taken on Gorytus showed nothing untoward, but that in turn does not conclusively rule out the existence of a drug which could not be found by the testing procedures in operation at that time. Whatever the reason for the run, there was no lasting harm to Gorytus. He was soon passed fit to return to the track as a three-year-old, an interesting prospect for Carson to consider that winter.

Carson ended the year on a stately high. In the New Year's Honours List he was awarded an OBE 'for services to racing': recognition for his contribution to the sport over the twenty years since he rode his first winner, Pinkers Pond. The lad from Stirling had indeed come a long way.

William Hunter Carson, OBE.
Willie after the investiture at Buckingham Palace in 1983

CHAPTER ELEVEN
TWO BRILLIANT FILLIES

The mystery of Gorytus's flop in the Dewhurst Stakes continued to perplex racing. No entirely satisfactory explanation had been found, but the colt was none the worse for his experience, outwardly at least.

Now Hern turned his attention to the forthcoming Classics. Gorytus would still be aimed at the 2,000 Guineas in an attempt to redeem his reputation. Again the fates turned against him. A better horse on fast ground, his preparation was hindered by an abnormally wet spring. So bad was the weather in the early months of the year that all three days of the Chester May meeting were washed out; fixtures were lost with clockwork regularity.

Hern had to settle for giving Gorytus racecourse gallops at Bath and Newmarket, so when Guineas day arrived there was no concrete evidence of Gorytus's well-being. But the noises from West Ilsley were encouraging, and it says plenty for the power of Gorytus's reputation that he started 7–2 second favourite for the first colts' Classic. Diesis, who had never received much credit for his Dewhurst win in view of the Gorytus controversy, led the market at 100–30.

Gorytus looked superb in the paddock and in the race he looked as though he was going to live up to his looks and his reputation. Two furlongs out Carson took the lead, driving for home. The crowd, sensing a remarkable victory in the offing, urged him forward. But it was a short-lived effort. Before the final furlong he had been overhauled, and slipped further back down the field as Lomond, trained by Vincent O'Brien and ridden by Pat Eddery, seized victory. Gorytus finished fifth, some four lengths behind the winner.

It had been a creditable performance, but one of a horse not quite up to the very highest class. His only two subsequent runs supported that assessment. Plagued by the wet weather, he did not run again until the Benson & Hedges Gold Cup at York in August when he finished two lengths fourth to the French Derby winner Caerleon, also trained by O'Brien. He bowed out with a fifth, beaten two and a half lengths, to Montekin in the Waterford Crystal Mile at Goodwood.

Gorytus's legacy was a string of unanswered questions. What really happened at Newmarket? Had he been got at? Was he suffering from the coughing in Hern's stable at that time? Did his three-year-old form show him to be what he was, a good but not top-class horse? Had the press and public, not for the first time or the last, simply gone overboard about a horse and been proved wrong? So many questions, so few answers. His races at three-year-old demonstrated he was below top class, but his admirers will always insist that something happened that day at Newmarket which prevented him fulfilling his seemingly limitless promise.

Carson was to enjoy a more fruitful association with his mount in the 1,000 Guineas, the John Dunlop-trained Habibti. She had won her three races as a two-year-old, but blotted her copybook when odds-on favourite for the Fred Darling Stakes at Newbury on her reappearance. After pulling hard early on, she could manage only third to Goodbye Shelley. Undeterred, Dunlop sent her to Newmarket. She ran well,

Sun Princess puts plenty of daylight between herself and her toiling pursuers in the 1983 Oaks

finishing fourth to the French-trained Ma Biche, without ever threatening to get to grips with the winner. 'She gave me a good ride but didn't stay the mile,' Carson reported.

Now Dunlop faced a dilemma. Should she be dropped back in distance, or should he have a crack at the Irish 1,000 Guineas? 'We decided to go to Ireland,' Dunlop recalls. 'There was that doubt about her stamina, but we thought that if she ran to her Newmarket form she would be good enough. In hindsight it was a mistake.' Habibti never showed in the race at the Curragh and finished well down the field behind another French filly, L'Attrayante. Although, as Dunlop admitted, it had been an error to go to Ireland, he now knew for certain that Habibti would be a sprinter.

With the endless heavy ground eventually ruling Gorytus out of the Derby, Carson was forced to rely on Morcon, the winner of the Predominate Stakes at Goodwood, as he sought a third blue riband. What a Derby day that was. There was a serious doubt about the meeting ever taking place, as, the night before, an almost apocalyptic storm broke over the south-east. Thunder detonated, lightning split the sky and rain simply poured onto the track.

The great day survived, just, but there was no happy ending for Carson. On a day made for mudlarks, Morcon finished eighth to Teenoso, Lester Piggott's ninth Derby winner. Carson did, however, have much higher hopes for a third Oaks triumph. Sun Princess, representing the Troy team of Sobell/Weinstock, Hern and Carson, had been given the archetypical stable preparation for a late maturing filly. One outing as a two-year-old and another in her second season, had seen Sun Princess finish second twice in useful company. But her potential was greater than the form figures suggested.

'Willie had always liked her,' Brian Procter, West Ilsley's chief work rider, relates. 'He had great faith that she would make a good filly. She needed time, but was beginning to come good. I rode her on the mile and a half gallop with three other horses, one of which was Little Wolf [who would win the Ascot Gold Cup for Carson]. She absolutely paralysed them. That was impressive because Little Wolf was a good yardstick at home. You had to be useful to get past him.'

Sun Princess started at 6-1 for the Oaks and those with the foresight to invest at that price never had a moment's doubt about collecting. After some jostling at the top of the hill, Carson made a decision. 'To hell with this, I'm getting out of here,' he admitted was his first thought. So he did. Quickening down Tattenham Hill, Sun Princess was in front half a mile out and drew further and further clear, leaving a Classic field strung out in her wake. At the line she was twelve lengths clear, with Carson having to peer over his shoulder to catch sight of the remainder.

Sun Princess was the first maiden to win a Classic of any description since Asmena won the Oaks in 1950. Better still, by putting twelve lengths between herself and the rest of the field she promised to set light to a season which had begun so miserably. Carson considered a while before placing Sun Princess in front of his two previous Oaks winners, Dunfermline and Bireme. 'I have to say she's the best of the three, because she not only stays as well as they did but she has more speed.'

Weinstock and Hern decided Sun Princess should miss the Irish Oaks in favour of the King George VI and Queen Elizabeth Diamond Stakes at Ascot seven weeks later. With Sun Princess's agenda set, Carson could turn his attention to Habibti. Dunlop had given her a rest after her defeat in the Irish Guineas and now had the July Cup at Newmarket, one of the season's premier sprints, pencilled in for her. 'She was in great heart after her break and we felt she was going to Newmarket with a real chance,' Dunlop says. 'The mile had been beyond her and this six furlongs looked like suiting her much better.'

The betting market reflected the stable confidence. Backed from 10-1 to 8-1, Habibti was a comfortable two and a half lengths winner from Soba, with Carson

*Carson after winning the Gold Cup at Ascot
on Little Wolf in 1983*

Willie receives the Ritz Club Trophy from the Queen Mother for the leading jockey at Royal Ascot in 1983

having to do little more than keep her up to her task. 'Brilliant, absolutely brilliant,' Carson said as he dismounted.

Carson's season had come alive with a vengeance. Having unearthed a top-class middle-distance horse in Sun Princess, he now had the prospective champion sprinter in his camp. Habibti's next race would be the William Hill Sprint Championship over five furlongs at York in August. Sun Princess was made 9–4 joint favourite for the King George with Caerleon, the winner of the Prix du Jockey-Club. Although Carson produced her to have every chance approaching the final furlong, she could never get to grips with the leaders, Time Charter and Diamond Shoal. Time Charter ran on strongly to beat Diamond Shoal by three-quarters of a length, with Sun Princess another length third. It was, after all, only her fourth race, and the first occasion on which she had raced against older horses. It was also her first race against the colts. She could be expected to learn from the experience, although for her next race, the Yorkshire Oaks, she reverted to solely female company.

Carson enjoyed a fine Ebor meeting at York. Sun Princess and Habibti were both successful, and he completed a big-race double for Dunlop with Seymour Hicks in the Great Voltigeur Stakes.

Plans now had to be laid for the big autumn prizes. Habibti would take the traditional sprinter's route: the Vernons Sprint Cup at Haydock, then on to the Prix de l'Abbaye de Longchamp on Arc day. But Sun Princess presented her connections with a problem: her objective would be the Arc, the race which Sobell and Weinstock so dearly wanted to win, but what would be the best preparation?

The choice was between the Prix Vermeille at Longchamp, a great race in itself, but equally significantly a recognised Arc trial for fillies, and the St Leger. Such

Habibti proves herself a top-class sprinter by beating Soba in the 1983 July Cup at Newmarket

was the intricacy of the decision that Habibti had already won the Vernons, more than two weeks after York, before an answer to the Sun Princess question was even in sight. Eventually it came: she would go to Doncaster.

Even then the dramas were not over. Soft ground threatened to force her withdrawal on the day of the race, so great was Weinstock's determination to avoid her endangering her Arc prospects by having a hard race. I remember Hern and Weinstock huddled together in the weighing room at Doncaster, Hern trying to impress upon Weinstock how much bad press he would attract by withdrawing a short-priced Classic favourite little more than minutes before the start.

Weinstock relented, and Sun Princess and Carson did the rest. The 11–8 favourite quickened magnificently entering the final furlong to beat Esprit Du Nord by three-quarters of a length. 'She didn't have a hard race,' Carson said. 'I rode her with the Arc in mind.' The roars from the crowd which erupted in the straight and again in the winner's enclosure left no doubt about their feelings. They had come to see a champion filly and would not have taken kindly to a last-minute defection.

'To have taken the filly out would have been bad for the St Leger and bad for racing,' Hern said. 'And it would have been unnecessary.' Simon Weinstock, despite Carson's assurance that he had taken good care of Sun Princess, was unrepentant about his reluctance to run. 'I was not at all keen,' he said. 'I'll let you know what I think in Paris in three weeks' time.'

Carson warmed up for the Arc with an electrifying victory on Habibti in the Prix de l'Abbaye. In beating Soba by a length, Habibti knocked a staggering 1.2 seconds off the five-furlong course record. Then came the moment of truth for Sun Princess.

The dry autumn had left the ground firmer than she would have liked, and there was the nagging query over the race at Doncaster and any after effects. In the event she ran a magnificent race. Joe Mercer did an excellent job on Sailors Dance of setting the gallop for Sun Princess. Sailors Dance held the lead until Sun Princess and Diamond Shoal, her adversary from the King George, attacked as the field turned for home. Now All Along was beginning to make progress. Diamond Shoal was the first to crack as Carson struck for home. But gallantly as the filly tried, she could not repel the late challenge of All Along and went down by a length. There was no room for recriminations among Sun Princess's connections. 'She ran a marvellous race,' Carson said. 'She could have done with easier ground but she was magnificent.'

Simon Weinstock had had his fears laid gloriously to rest. 'The race in the St Leger did her no harm at all,' he said. 'She's finished racing now and will be retired to Ballymacoll Stud.' Once again the glittering prize had eluded Hern and Carson, but there was no despondency as they travelled home from France. From the season's stuttering beginning they had developed a splendid filly who had provided some spectacular moments and only narrowly failed to secure the Arc.

Despite the efforts of Sun Princess and Habibti, there were times when Carson seemed to spend more time out of the saddle than in it. A season-long struggle with the stewards was to cost an astonishing twenty-six days in suspensions, comprised of three individual bans. With the year barely under way, Carson received a portent of how his season would unfold. At Ayr on 28 March, just the fourth day of the new campaign, he was given a six-day suspension for careless riding. Mendick Adventure, his mount in the Kidsneuk Maiden Stakes, was adjudged by the stewards to have interfered with Rosinka, who finished second to Special Fruit.

Carson was incensed. 'That's the first time I've ever been banned for keeping straight,' he said. 'The gap was there for me to go through but Alan Mercer [the rider of Rosinka] took out his whip and she began to roll across the course.' Denys Smith, the experienced and much respected trainer of Mendick Adventure, agreed with Carson. 'Willie was not to blame,' he said, 'it was the second horse which was at fault. I stand by my jockey.'

The ban, although hardly the ideal way to start the season, was more than anything an irritant. Carson would miss no big meetings and indeed returned for the opening day of Newmarket's Craven meeting, the first significant fixture on the Flat. But it had planted in his mind a sense of injustice which would return to dog him.

It was 30 July, and the final day of the Glorious Goodwood meeting, when Carson next felt the stewards' wrath. He was suspended for eight days, again for careless riding, when his mount Air Distingué was beaten by Acclimatise in the Nassau Stakes. Once more Carson was stung by what he believed to be an aberration on the part of the officials. 'That was not careless riding, I don't care what they say,' he said. Despite his protestations the stewards' decision stood. Air Distingué was disqualified and now he totalled fourteen days spent on the sidelines.

Worse was to come. The following month he travelled north to Beverley in Yorkshire to ride the two-year-old filly Shuteye, trained by Hern, the last race on the card. Shuteye won by two and a half lengths after some scrimmaging two furlongs out. Not thinking that anything might be amiss, he left the course immediately after the race. The Beverley stewards, having watched a replay of the race, decided they wanted to interview the by-now absent Carson. They notified him that they would hold an enquiry into the race on his next venture north. His case, meanwhile, had not been helped by the assertion of the apprentice jockey Chris Coates, the rider of third-placed Fill The Jug, that he 'had been murdered' by Carson and Shuteye.

Carson met the stewards two weeks later when he rode at York. He was adjudged to have been responsible for the interference when Shuteye dived left a quarter of a mile from home, and once more careless riding was the verdict. This time, though, as it was his third offence, he was referred to the Jockey Club's Portman Square headquarters in London for sentence. Carson's cool dissolved. 'All the other jockeys in the race say I was clear,' he stormed. Carson reserved his strongest vitriol for the officials. 'How can they send me to Portman Square on this evidence?' he asked. A parting shot could not be resisted: 'They must think all jockeys are liars.'

With the jockeys' championship battle now reaching a critical point, the stewards' findings were awaited with heightened interest. On the day Carson attended Portman Square he led Piggott by eighteen winners, 152 to 134. Although the season had little more than three weeks to run, if Carson received a hefty ban and Piggott scented the possibility of closing the gap, the title could be thrown wide open.

The stewards suspended Carson for twelve days, effective from the next day. He flew by helicopter to Warwick to see Piggott ride one winner. Even with Carson sidelined Piggott conceded the enormity of his task. 'It will be pretty difficult to catch him,' he said. But if anyone could, Piggott was the man. Carson was in for an uncomfortable spell. The final weeks of the season are always the most difficult time to accumulate winners. Large fields of often moderate horses produce surprise results, making the doubles and trebles Piggott required hard to find. He could never build up sufficient momentum and Carson's advantage remained secure.

While he was forced to sit and watch Piggott doing his utmost, Carson had time, and plenty of it, to mull over what was becoming a remarkable season. The bans had cost him in the region of £10,000 but he was more troubled by the way his faith in Jockey Club justice was draining away. 'I'm numb,' he said. 'It seems incredible that when somebody else breaks the rules you get the blame. But if you live in a dictatorship you have to do what the dictators say. Beverley was just too ludicrous. The penalties now are so severe they might as well send us to prison. Some of us are losing respect for the stewards. Sometimes you feel as though you might as well talk to a wall. I've already missed a seventh of the season. One little nudge and I could be off again.'

Carson's outburst was more prescient than his worst nightmare could have imagined. On the day of his return he rode My Aisling at Nottingham. They finished first but, incredibly, the stewards again considered Carson guilty of careless riding and demoted My Aisling to third. Carson was once more on his way to Portman Square. 'London again,' he said resignedly. 'It was an accident and again it wasn't my fault.' The jockey did at least have the consolation of completing a double which effectively put the title beyond Piggott's reach. He now stood at 154 winners, ten more than Piggott.

When Carson's case was heard, the stewards of the Jockey Club disciplinary committee concurred with Carson. Although they confirmed the decision of the Nottingham stewards in placing My Aisling third, they absolved Carson of any blame. As we spoke after the hearing, Carson's relief was palpable. The shadow of a fourth suspension had been banished, but the strain he had been feeling was plain, as a muscle in his cheek twitched involuntarily. 'Of course I've been depressed,' he said. 'You always are at times like these. But this time it's been particularly bad. It was as though someone had it in for me. I suppose I upset a lot of people with what I said after the Beverley business, but it's difficult to keep quiet when your livelihood is at stake and you know you're in the right.'

While Carson was firing off broadsides at the stewards, his disposition had not been helped by criticism of some of his own attitudes. As the season drew to a close, every fixture was vital as he and Piggott battled neck and neck for the jockeys' title. Tom Wilson, then the chairman of the Musselburgh Joint Racing Committee, saw a shining opportunity to raise the profile of his course, Edinburgh. The track held two end of season meetings, and with Carson and Piggott locked together Wilson saw the chance to draw two of the top names in the sport.

He decided to approach Carson first, appealing to his Scottish background and suggesting that Carson might like to put something back into racing in Scotland. 'He refused because he said the course was too dangerous,' Wilson says. 'I told him that there had been only one accident at Edinburgh in fourteen years. Then I asked whether, as he was so concerned about safety, he would ride again at York, where he had his bad accident. I was very disappointed with his attitude. I felt he had turned his back on Scotland and his Scottish heritage.' For someone who has spent a large part of his professional life carrying such epithets as 'the irrepressible Scot' and 'the Flying Scot', Carson has a detached view of his native land. He considers blue his favourite colour 'perhaps because of the Scottish flag' yet apparently has little desire to spend much time in Scotland.

Wilson is not alone in his views. The journalist Tom McConnell, a keen follower of sport in Scotland and the author of *The Tartan Turf*, views Carson as a less than enthusiastic Scotsman. 'Although he is a Scot, he thinks we are a lot of moaning minnies,' McConnell says. 'He is very much an Anglicised Scot. He has been down there so long he regards himself as English. He found success in England and now doesn't come up here when he's not working because the weather isn't good enough. Scottish punters idolise him, yet there are times when he feels that whenever he comes to Scotland they give him a bad time.'

Carson's case is not without foundation. He quotes the instance of being thrown from the favourite in a race at Ayr and returning to the weighing room to a barrage of rubbish thrown by the spectators. 'Scottish racegoers are the worst in the world,' he would say after that incident. 'They don't know how to behave.'

David McHarg, the general manager at Ayr racecourse and one of the leading figures in Scottish racing, is more charitable. 'It is true we don't see much of him in Scotland but I wonder if I would be any different in his position,' he says. 'Willie has never been one for the smaller meetings – he doesn't have to be. There is a special atmosphere at Scottish tracks. The punters create it, they're very voluble. The crowd

Reluctant wearer of the tartan? Carson on the gallops in 1974

can often give the rider on a beaten favourite a hard time, and Willie doesn't like that. Willie has never been short of a wisecrack but up here he tends to get them all back.'

But, Edinburgh or not, suspensions or not, the figures showed that Carson had amassed 159 winners by the end of the season, nine more than Piggott and enough to collect his fifth and, so far, last jockeys' championship. The margin would, of course, have been much wider had officialdom not taken such a dim view of Carson's efforts. As he said: 'It would have been cruel to lose a title I deserved.'

CHAPTER TWELVE
DESPAIR

Carson began the 1984 season in the highest spirits; he ended it in the deepest gloom. A fifth championship, Classic wins on Sun Princess and his association with the fleet Habibti had given him the perfect platform for another successful campaign.

How quickly fortunes can change. For the first time since 1970 he failed to ride 100 winners, a broken wrist received in a fall in Milan restricting his total to ninety-seven. Nor could Habibti revive him. She reappeared with an emphatic win in a minor race at Lingfield and looked set for a new triumphal march when taking the King's Stand Stakes at Royal Ascot by a short head from Anita's Prince. That was her last success. Five unsuccessful runs followed and she was retired to stud. 'She was very good at Lingfield and I thought we were off again,' John Dunlop recalls. 'But between then and Ascot she developed an unusual muscular condition and was never the same again.' Dunlop did, however, provide a rare bright spot for Carson when the Arundel-trained Circus Plume won the Yorkshire Oaks at York's big August meeting.

I stayed as usual at West Ilsley for the Royal Ascot meeting. On the Tuesday morning, the first day of the four-day fixture, I went to the gallops to watch three horses being given pipe-openers for Ascot. Hern keenly watched the proceedings from his hack as a handsome bay colt, the picture of vitality, came pounding up the gallops. 'Head For Heights is very well,' he said sharply from under his brown velvet cap.

As the string moved away he turned his hack to follow them. It was the last time I saw him on a horse. On 7 December that year Hern broke his neck in a hunting accident in Leicestershire. 'They were jumping a fence and couldn't see what was on the other side,' said Sheilah Hern, describing the accident. 'In front of them was a stone water trough and the horse tried to take avoiding action by jinking in mid-air. It stumbled to its knees on landing and fired my husband off.' The following day he was moved to Stoke Mandeville Hospital and, partially paralysed, he was in traction for six weeks. After an operation on 13 February, the trainer made his first visit to West Ilsley the following month and was discharged in April. Though confined to a wheelchair, he has never lost control of stable operations.

Hern's recovery surprised even those used to the resilience of the human spirit in the face of towering adversity. After six months he could walk with assistance from either side, and by then he was supervising the work of his horses from his red Mercedes station wagon. When staying for Goodwood at Leet D'Arcy, the Herns' holiday home at West Wittering, the trainer still spent a couple of hours a day walking slowly and painfully around the lawn with the help of Marcus Tregoning, an assistant trainer. A set of parallel bars hammered into the lawn was further evidence of his determination to continue his treatment. 'Dr Frankel at Stoke Mandeville told me that most people with my condition would have to take a year off,' Hern said. 'I replied that that was quite impossible, and that if I did I would have to retire. I have no intention of doing that.'

Speculation had been rife that week that the trainer would go racing at Goodwood

Habibti (far side) gets up in the very last stride to pip Anitas Prince
in the King's Stand Stakes at Royal Ascot in 1984

for the first time since his accident. Hern, however, had thoughts only of his recovery. 'It would be a great mistake to do so at this stage,' he said. 'I have a two-hour physio session every day at home and also go in the swimming pool. What with watching work, looking at the horses and getting all the paperwork done, I have no time for anything else. If I started to go racing again I would have to drop the physio. I can't do that as I'm determined to assist my recovery in every way.'

Sheilah, Hern's tireless wife, was a tower of strength. Alternately bullying and encouraging, she kept the wheels turning as smoothly as possible, even though the strain of so doing was obviously becoming almost intolerable. To add to their problems, the horses had been out of sorts, having contracted some unknown virus. Having been almost put out of business by the dreaded scourge in his early days in Berkshire, Hern was well aware of this particular nightmare. 'The virus is like a thief in the night,' he said. 'You don't see it coming and you don't see it go. This time there were no other symptoms, except for a lack of zest in the horses. Then suddenly after a long lean spell, they were running their races out as they should.'

Despite his infirmity, the vitality of spirit that had helped to keep Hern at the top of such an often ruthless business was still intact. 'The one thing I miss is riding out with the string,' he said. 'I like to be able to observe the horses, to see whether they are sweating and how they've taken their work. Whether they are enjoying themselves or whether they are starting to think a bit. I like to see them both before, during and after their work.'

The rare bright spots in West Ilsley's dark summer were provided by Helen Street and Petoski. Helen Street won the Irish Oaks, but it was Petoski who was the stable's saviour. The three-year-old belonged to Lady Beaverbrook, for so many years such a distinctive figure and intrepid bidder at the yearling sales. Petoski, a useful two-year-old, shaped promisingly on his reappearance when runner-up in both the Sandown Classic Trial and the Chester Vase. He ran below par in the Derby at a time when the stable was out of form, finishing eleventh behind Slip Anchor. At the Newmarket July meeting, Willie rode the colt to a thoroughly satisfactory win in the Princess of Wales' Stakes, but Petoski's effort hardly suggested that he was about to vanquish most of the best horses in Europe in the King George VI and Queen Elizabeth Diamond Stakes at Ascot.

Despite the three-year-old's starting price of 12–1 Petoski's victory came as no

An old alliance successfully renewed: Carson takes the 1984 Queen Elizabeth II Stakes at Ascot on Lord Derby's Teleprompter

*Carson (right) on Petoski wins the King George VI and Queen Elizabeth
Diamond Stakes from Oh So Sharp (left) at Ascot in 1985*

surprise to the camp. 'I remember we galloped him on the trial ground,' says
Tregoning, 'and at the usual conference afterwards Brian Procter said, "This horse
will win". So we all backed him.' By common consent, Carson put up one of his
finest riding performances in that year's running of Britain's most important all-
aged race. A high-class field included Henry Cecil's subsequent Triple Crown winning
filly, Oh So Sharp, Vincent O'Brien's Irish Derby winner, Law Society, and Jeremy
Tree's Rainbow Quest, who that autumn was to be awarded the Prix de l'Arc de
Triomphe on the disqualification of Sagace.

Law Society and Pat Eddery were always struggling to hold their position. Oh
So Sharp, despite being hampered by Infantry early in the straight, looked all set
for victory when Steve Cauthen kicked for home below the distance. Carson had
been pumping away for a long time, apparently getting nowhere until, after switching
Petoski to the outside, he drove the colt past the filly in the final strides to win his
third King George and also to give Hern a record fourth win.

Eddery, eventually fourth on Law Society, paid tribute to Carson. 'We were getting
nowhere and Oh So Sharp looked a certainty when Steve kicked to the front, but
when Willie switched Petoski to the outside they fairly flew.' Carson also thought
he was entitled to the accolades. 'The King George is a bit of a law unto itself.
Normally you have to lie close to the pace over the Ascot mile and a half because
of the short home straight. But when they've gone a good gallop you can come from
a very long way back and wait as long as you want, as I did on Petoski. He was
a very underrated horse and on that day one of the best I've ever ridden.' Cauthen,

however, was not convinced. 'Willie had been bashing away for a long time getting nowhere. The ground was too firm for Oh So Sharp and she just tied up in the last furlong.'

The amount of work that Hern was putting in towards his recovery was astonishing. He was, if anything, trying too hard, a fact unhappily illustrated when he fell off a wooden horse on which he was exercising and broke his thigh at the beginning of October. But thanks to the exploits of Petoski, Hern kept his position in the top half-dozen trainers, finishing sixth behind Henry Cecil in the table. Carson, who had also enjoyed a respectable season, rode 125 winners and finished third to Eddery in the jockeys' championship.

Carson's vociferously expressed loyalty to Hern has been a recurring theme of their relationship, but as the pressure bore down on him the depressive side of his nature

LEFT *Longboat wins the 1986 Gold Cup at Ascot*

OPPOSITE *Returning to the winner's enclosure at Ascot on Longboat*

began to overpower the optimist. At a dinner party during Royal Ascot, the dark side won. Guests were shocked to hear him say gloomily, 'The old man's gone; I don't know what's going to become of us all.'

Talking about those bad times, Lord Weinstock said, 'It's no surprise that Willie should have become demoralised at that time. Look at what happened to Dick during that period. After his accident, he had a prostate operation. Then he fell and broke his thigh. Then in 1988 he had heart surgery. It's a wonder he survived at all, let alone continued at the top of the tree.'

For West Ilsley, the only highlights of 1986 were achieved with Longboat as Dick Hollingsworth's fine stayer landed the treble of the Ascot Gold Cup, and the Goodwood and Doncaster Cups. The 1986 season will always be remembered as the

year of Dancing Brave. Khalid Abdullah's champion, unluckily defeated by Shahrastani in the Derby, had earlier won the 2,000 Guineas. The Guy Harwood-trained colt then went on to win the Eclipse, the King George and the Arc. For once Willie was a bystander on these great occasions. But despite the shortage of Group One wins he still managed to finish third to Pat Eddery in the jockeys' championship, with 130 winners.

Paradoxically, 1987, which saw Carson universally acclaimed for his brilliant riding of Don't Forget Me in the 2,000 Guineas, also saw the rider sink deeper into despair as the season progressed. His mood reached its lowest ebb as Cauthen and Eddery fought out their dramatic battle for the jockeys' title.

Don't Forget Me, trained by Richard Hannon, had been not far below the top flight as a two-year-old. His three wins from four starts included victories in the Lanson Champagne Vintage Stakes at Goodwood and the Laurent Perrier Champagne Stakes at Doncaster. When Don't Forget Me reappeared in the Craven Stakes at Newmarket, Carson rode John Dunlop's Love The Groom, who was outpaced before finishing fourth. Up front, a tremendous battle developed between Eddery on Don't Forget Me and Walter Swinburn on Ajdal. Showing superior speed, Ajdal went ahead in the dip, but, fighting back like a tiger, Don't Forget Me was only three-quarters of a length adrift at the line. But hopes were high at Hannon's Wiltshire base that these placings would be reversed in the stronger gallop of the 2,000 Guineas. Don't Forget Me belonged to John Horgan. And the cattle baron, from County Cork, together with his brothers had already plunged on their pride and joy at 66–1. With Eddery required to ride Bellotto through his retainer for Khalid Abdullah, Carson had been booked for the Hannon-trained colt.

Disaster nearly struck the day before. When travelling up from Wiltshire on the Friday the colt spread a plate and bruised his off fore foot. The news spread as accounts of the injury became more and more alarming. Neither Hannon nor his staff got much sleep. Don't Forget Me had five hours of solid treatment including the constant application of ice packs. Even then it was not certain whether the colt would run or not until the moment he entered the stalls. Carson, who had only been booked on the Monday, was under instructions to withdraw the colt if he felt him go the slightest bit lame. Despite this, the team were full of confidence and the Horgans went in again when Don't Forget Me drifted to 10–1. Carson excelled himself, breaking smartly from the stalls and making every yard of the running. Ajdal, Midyan and Deputy Governor all attacked in turn, and on the hill Eddery and Bellotto came storming up the slope to be beaten by only a neck.

It had been a rough race. The stewards had to enquire into three separate incidents. In a wind-assisted 1 minute 36.74 seconds, Don't Forget Me had covered the Rowley Mile in the fastest time recorded in the Classic since My Babu in 1948. The normal pattern for a race is for the pace to be at its hottest in the third quarter, with the runners slowing down as they tire in the closing stages. But this time, reflecting Carson's marvellous judgement, the gallop increased steadily throughout. The final quarter was run in 22.75 seconds compared with the 25.06 seconds for the first quarter. Carson had shown an acute tactical sense. Acknowledging this, Eddery says, 'He rode a marvellous race. Everybody talks about these American jockeys coming over with clocks in their heads. But here you've got a straight mile at Newmarket and a wide open track. Yet he jumped off and made all. He paced himself well.'

A tidal wave of emotion engulfed the Newmarket unsaddling enclosure as Carson rode back in triumph. Eight of the twelve Horgan brothers and sisters, together with three plane-loads of relations and friends, had given their heroes a Cheltenham-like welcome. The reception was even more deafening at the Curragh on 18 May when Carson and Don't Forget Me gave a repeat performance of their Newmarket win. Ajdal was again made favourite at 6–4, but flattered only to deceive, finishing fourth.

Don't Forget Me failed to win again, his disappointments curiously mirroring Carson's own decline. Never had I seen Willie so discontented. Fleet Street, normally indifferent to racing, sent their star sports reporters all over the country as the enthralling battle between Cauthen and Eddery reached its climax. Carson was ignored, relegated to the chorus from which he had spent so many years struggling to escape. He managed to ride 100 winners, but it was a poor total by his standards, and he was visibly upset by the adulation given to his rivals. In addition, for part of this period he had been forbidden to talk to the media or to go on television. This order had been issued to protect the jockey from embarrassing situations when Hern was absent through illness.

This was a mistake, as lack of communication breeds further misunderstandings. Now, denied the spotlight of television and deprived of the limelight by his rivals, he made no attempt to woo or placate his critics. I tried to reason with him and point out that the media also possess egos which need massaging. A little politeness goes a long way. He could not see it, and the media became increasingly resentful. The two sides grew more intractable, like two armies grimly trying to stare each other down. In retaliation, Carson's anger became more and more evident as he defiantly pushed his five foot, 7st 10lb frame through the uncaring crowds outside the weighing room.

More than any other rider, Carson, who can become surprisingly introverted, needs constant big-time success to boost his adrenalin. 'When I wanted help from the press I didn't get it,' he complained. 'I wasn't riding winners and I started making mistakes so they went for my jugular.' Interestingly, Eddery remained Carson's chief advocate. 'Never forget Willie,' he said. 'He's as good as any of us. He's just not getting the breaks at the moment.'

As the season drew to a close, there were signs of better things in store. Emmson, having wound up a successful two-year-old campaign by beating Sheriff's Star and Salse in the William Hill Futurity, was one of the winter favourites for the Derby. Minster Son, Unfuwain and Charmer were other promising colts. The tide was at last beginning to turn.

CHAPTER THIRTEEN
OUT OF THE DARKNESS

One of the most revealing remarks ever made by Willie Carson was when sitting in his Mercedes outside Newbury racecourse in the spring of 1988. 'As long as the Major's still got good horses for me to ride and I'm still enjoying the game I'll be there. I'd go through hell and high water for Dick Hern because I'm wanted. To be wanted is the most important thing in life.'

Mike Cattermole, Carson's agent, put the relationship in a nutshell. 'They are two very different people from very different backgrounds. But there is a strong mutual respect between them. Willie is 100 per cent behind the Major because he knows the Major is 100 per cent behind him. They are both willing listeners to each other. From a professional point of view it's a very good relationship.'

Having been inculcated with a strong sense of self-discipline and self-motivation from an early age, Carson has developed a shrewd understanding of the Major's way with men and horses. 'The military thing shows through all the time,' he said. 'The Major is a 1930s man. It's all about discipline and loyalty and getting on with the job. He's got everyone doing what he wants and he doesn't have to keep on telling them,' said the jockey.

Michael Stoute, himself a successful trainer, once said that the narrowest dividing line in life is that between the winners and the nearly winners. Both Hern and Carson are supreme winners, and, vitally, survivors. They are both also imaginative. This helps Carson to understand what is going on inside a horse's mind. 'Only the real athletes, the top horses, are automatic runners,' he once said. 'They've got big hearts and good limbs. It doesn't hurt them. The ordinary horse has to have this certain element of fear to make it go. Lots of horses have problems you don't see and it hurts them to go faster. You have to growl and whack them to make them go through the pain barrier.'

Above all, Hern's love of good things, of a bottle of champagne and of singing, are legendary. And for the first time for years, there seemed to be plenty to sing about in the spring of 1988 at West Ilsley. Derby candidates abounded with Unfuwain, Charmer, Emmson and Minster Son a quartet of likely contenders. The problems confronting Willie as he pondered his Derby mount were even more daunting than usual, especially with his 100 per cent record of making the correct choice. In 1979, he had preferred Troy to Milford, and a year later discarded Water Mill in favour of Henbit.

Unfuwain, an impeccably bred son of Northern Dancer and Height Of Fashion, had romped home in soft ground at Epsom and Chester, proving his ability to handle the Derby course and stay a mile and a half. Emmson, the winner the previous season of the William Hill Futurity, had been slow to come to hand, but had run well when third in the Mecca-Dante Stakes. Charmer, owned by Lady Beaverbrook, had made good progress from two to three years and had surprised everyone when finishing a close second to Doyoun in the 2,000 Guineas. Minster Son, bred at Carson's Minster Stud in Gloucestershire, was very much a contender for the jockey's services, having embarrassed everyone by beating the more fancied Unfuwain at Newbury the previous autumn. The jockey's pride and joy had already made a winning reappearance when conceding 3 lb to Red Glow, the Derby favourite, at Newmarket.

Like Charmer, Minster Son belonged to Lady Beaverbrook, having been sold for 36,000 guineas at the Newmarket sales. A comedy of errors, or more likely a case of wilful misunderstanding by the indomitable Lady Beaverbrook, had taken place at the auction.

Lord Chelsea had been anxious to buy a yearling and place it with Major Hern, who had told him that Minster Son was a nice type of horse. Unfortunately, Lady Beaverbrook had also said that she was interested in the same animal. So a complicated plan was devised whereby Lady Beaverbrook was to take over the bidding if the pace became too hot for Lord Chelsea, who was only prepared to go to 17,000 guineas. Of course, in no time at all, the two parties were at each others throats. Lord Chelsea eventually gave best as the hammer fell to Lady Beaverbrook's bid of 36,000 guineas.

Carson weighed the options, but his thoughts strayed continually down the same tracks. 'Minster Son,' he mused. 'I know Red Glow improved when winning at York, but it was Minster Son's first race of the season as well. He could be a bottomless tank. Charmer? Was the Guineas form good enough? Will he stay? Unfuwain? He's a lovely galloping horse and he acts on any ground. But there's one snag, he doesn't seem able to change gear quickly. Emmson? Could improve on York, but will the race come too soon?' Round and round he went, but still that leaning toward Minster Son persisted.

One morning at West Ilsley, the discussion became so heated that the four of us – Dick and Sheilah, Carson and myself – wrote our ideas of the jockey's likely mount on pieces of paper, folded them up and put them in a silver cup on top of a cupboard. Months later we discovered that Carson had gone for Minster Son, the colt he eventually chose after winning the Predominate Stakes at Goodwood.

123

Before the Derby, I went to watch the horses work at West Ilsley. It was a revelation to watch how Hern had adjusted to his disability. In 1985, the trainer had said how much he missed being able to ride with his horses. And now, three years later, his brain had devised a substitute. As Carson put it, 'Dick's eyes have become his hands.' It was an extraordinary experience sitting in his station wagon as the horses silently circle the vehicle to be scrutinised by the trainer after their morning work.

The Queen's racing manager Lord Carnarvon, who was later to become such a key figure in the drama over the lease at West Ilsley, had been a fascinated spectator. 'I sometimes feel that Dick sees more now than when he was riding horses and was able to touch their skins and feel their legs. He has always had an extraordinary ability to concentrate, and now when the lads ride the horses round him, he can see how they are breathing and how they have taken their exercise.'

The trainer's meticulous attention to detail and his keen powers of observation had always stood him in good stead. 'The moment their fast work is finished, his eyes are on the far downs watching them come back,' Lord Carnarvon went on. 'He'll see if a horse isn't trotting right or if it isn't relaxed. And he's always had this knack of noticing things that might go wrong.'

Carson, of course, had to shoulder plenty of extra responsibility. Discussing his feelings about his employer, he said: 'He's the most loyal person to a jockey I've ever known. His jockey is a part of his team and it's as if you are as one. You've got to be better with that sort of belief in you. It's total, total, total. He's not like other people. If I ride a bad race, that's it. Nothing is ever said, but we both know. It could even happen in a big race, but it's less likely because of the confidence that you've got in him.'

That year's Derby was not decided by any question of jockeyship on the part of Hern's riders. They all ran disappointingly, Unfuwain, Minster Son and Charmer finishing seventh, eighth and eleventh respectively behind Kahyasi. Minster Son's jockey–breeder was naturally dejected. 'He seemed to find the ground too firm,' said Carson.

During Royal Ascot, further disaster struck the Herns when the trainer had to undergo heart surgery. Once again the ship was without a rudder. This time, something had to be done. Alex Scott, the assistant trainer was leaving to start his own career. Neil Graham, at that time working for John Gosden in California had agreed to come as his replacement. But it now became a matter of urgency. 'I was due to come later on in the year,' says Graham, 'but I got a phone call from Sheilah asking me to come straight away.'

The normal veil of secrecy descended over the question of the Major's condition. As far as the outside world was concerned, life was going on as normal at West Ilsley with Hern's staff carrying out their usual duties and Graham and Marcus Tregoning supervising operations. But behind the scenes fears for the Major's life were being expressed. And as the trainer's lease from the Queen on West Ilsley stables was due to expire at the end of 1989, Lord Carnarvon and the Queen's advisers were becoming

*Carson and Chilibang after winning
the King's Stand Stakes at Royal Ascot in 1988,
to most people's amazement*

Unfuwain wins the 1988
Princess of Wales' Stakes at Newmarket
by fifteen lengths

increasingly worried about the future. So too was Mrs Hern and the trainer's many loyal friends and allies.

The Newmarket July meeting came and went. Unfuwain gave the stable yet another victory in the Princess of Wales' Stakes when storming home by fifteen lengths and would next take on Mtoto in the King George at Ascot. The rain that was expected

126

to help Unfuwain's cause came in time and the ground was good to soft. This was supposed to be against Mtoto, who had just won his second Eclipse Stakes for Sheikh Hamdan Al Maktoum's brother, Sheikh Ahmed, and Alec Stewart.

Michael Roberts, Mtoto's jockey, was a brilliant tactician and knew just how to exploit the colt's finishing speed to telling effect. 'Alec Stewart told me not to worry about being too far back. He said that Willie would try and slip the field later than

Unfuwain has no answer to Mtoto's finishing speed
in the 1988 King George VI
and Queen Elizabeth Stakes at Ascot

I thought and to ride my normal waiting race,' said Roberts. Stewart was right. Carson waited until early in the straight before making his move. Unfuwain ran on gamely, but had no answer to Mtoto's dazzling powers of acceleration.

At Goodwood, Carson was delighted when Minster Son returned to his best, beating Assatis and Alwuhush in the Gordon Stakes. The colt immediately became a strong

*Winning the St Leger at Doncaster, on Minster Son from
Diminuendo in 1988. Carson bred Minster Son himself*

fancy for the St Leger. At the beginning of September it was announced that Neil
Graham was to become caretaker/trainer for the rest of the season. The official line
was propounded by Sheilah Hern, who said that the doctors had ordered Hern to
take a complete rest for two months. It was emphasised that this move had nothing
to do with the Jockey Club and that it had been done at Hern's request. Not much

LEFT *Carson punches the air in triumph after Nashwan's Derby victory* (All-Sport)

BELOW *Nashwan's Epsom win gives Carson and Dick Hern, the trainer, plenty to smile about* (Tony Edenden)

ABOVE *Nashwan (far right) is poised to challenge the outsider Top Class as the field turns for home in the 1989 King George VI and Queen Elizabeth Stakes at Ascot* (Gerry Cranham)

RIGHT *Nashwan (left) holds off Cacoethes on the run to the line in the King George* (Trevor Jones)

OPPOSITE *Carson receives his winning trophy from the Queen after the King George* (Trevor Jones)

ABOVE *From apparently certain triumph, as Dayjur begins to overhaul Safely Kept in the Breeders' Cup Sprint at Belmont . . .* (Trevor Jones)

LEFT *. . . to disaster as he jumps a shadow, loses his momentum, and the race* (Phil Smith)

ABOVE *Shadayid gives Carson his sixteenth English Classic win in the 1991 1,000 Guineas at Newmarket*
(Gerry Cranham)

RIGHT *The triumphs continue . . . Marju defeats Desert Sun (No. 2) in the 1991 Craven Stakes at Newmarket*
(Gerry Cranham)

ABOVE *At home at his Minster Stud in Gloucestershire with wife Elaine* (Katz Pictures)

LEFT *Another call, another ride. The demand for Carson's services is as great as ever* (Katz Pictures)

RIGHT *Off we go again. Carson bursts from the stalls in the blue colours of Hamdan Al Maktoum, his chief retainer* (All-Sport)

BELOW *Willie Carson in the Queen's colours* (Gerry Cranham)

more was said at the time, but it was clear that a great deal was going on behind the scenes.

Although Graham's name was on the licence, Hern still kept in close touch with the daily running of the stable. The stricken trainer's refusal to knuckle under to his illness was almost beyond belief. Even from his hospital bed in the Cromwell Road, he was still issuing instructions about galloping and running plans to his equally determined wife, Sheilah, and to Marcus Tregoning.

Carson, largely a spectator as the dramas unfolded, had a marvellous time at Doncaster, where Prince Of Dance won the Champagne Stakes and Minster Son the St Leger. Prince Of Dance's two lengths defeat of Shining Steel gave Carson his 100th winner of the season for the seventeenth time in the past eighteen years.

The St Leger was a magnificent race to watch. Diminuendo, the Oaks winner, was a short-priced favourite at 4–7 to win the final Classic for Sheikh Mohammed and Henry Cecil. Walter Swinburn rode the filly, as Steve Cauthen had had a serious fall at Goodwood at the end of August. The moment of truth came over two furlongs from home, as Carson sent Minster Son into overdrive with both Diminuendo and Sheriff's Star queueing up to challenge. But Minster Son stayed on too strongly for the favourite, to win by a length.

What a moment it was for Carson to become the first jockey to breed and ride a Classic winner. Afterwards, wearing an outsize brown velvet jockey's cap, Carson insisted that Minster Son was a much underrated horse. 'He's not quite a Troy in that he's more of a galloper. But once he gets his head in front he's a difficult horse to beat,' he said. Pat Eddery saw immediately that Carson had played his hand perfectly. 'Willie made the right move when kicking for home such a long way out. He beat a better horse, because he saw to it that Minster Son outstayed her. He rode a great race.'

Acute observers of the scene noted that Sheilah Hern hung back from the celebrations. Although the pair had bowed to the inevitable when Graham was appointed caretaker, both the trainer and his wife were bitterly disappointed that their seventh victory in the Classic will never belong to them in the record books.

It continued to be a golden autumn for the stable with the twenty-eight-year-old Graham nominally in charge. The promising Nashwan won at Ascot in October, and Prince Of Dance followed up his Champagne Stakes win when dead heating with Scenic for the Dewhurst Stakes. A stewards' enquiry was ordered into the Dewhurst, but after a long delay the placings remained unaltered. The head-on camera patrol film showed that Scenic had veered towards Prince Of Dance inside the last furlong and had slightly brushed the favourite. The authorities took the view that it had been a case of two tired horses rolling under pressure. But for once Carson had made an error of judgement. With his usual frankness he had announced that the result had not been affected. A subsequent study of the film showed that the

Carson wearing the St Leger cap
after his triumph on Minster Son

Elaine congratulates Willie
after Minster Son's St Leger success

jockey could have been wrong, and Prince Of Dance might well have been awarded
the race outright.

In Paris, on the first Sunday in October, Unfuwain once again ran his heart out
to finish fourth to Tony Bin and Mtoto in the Arc. And at Doncaster later in the
month, an impressive victory by Al Hareb in the William Hill Futurity Stakes
apparently put the West Ilsley team in the driving seat for the 1989 Classics, with
Nashwan and Prince Of Dance also likely to prove live contenders.

Although Graham was officially credited with the winner, Hern had been back
at home for a fortnight and was firmly in the driving seat again. 'Al Hareb looks
an ideal Guineas type,' Hern said. 'I haven't had such a good hand for a long time.'
Carson, his 130 winners a big improvement on the bare century of a year ago, nodded
his agreement.

CHAPTER FOURTEEN
NASHWAN

Jockeys are sustained by riding good horses. More than simply winning, they crave the feeling of strength and power beneath them; literally, the horsepower. Willie Carson has experienced that sublime feeling often. Since High Top gave him his first Classic success in the 1972 2,000 Guineas, he has been associated with an impressive list of top-class horses, most of them during his enduring term as stable jockey to Dick Hern at West Ilsley.

Dunfermline, the gallant filly who won the Oaks and St Leger for the Queen in her Silver Jubilee year, 1977; Troy, who came from an apparently impossible position to win the 1979 Derby with an electrifying burst of acceleration; Henbit, that model of gallantry who took the 1980 Derby despite breaking down on the run to the post; Sun Princess, Rose Bowl, Habibti, Dibidale; the list goes on. Yet even that glorious roll call was to be topped. In 1989, Carson found Nashwan, a chestnut colt who was to carry the jockey to even greater heights.

Nashwan's formidable record, the only horse to win the 2,000 Guineas, the Derby, the Eclipse Stakes and the King George VI and Queen Elizabeth Diamond Stakes in the same season, tells only part of the story. For Carson, just being around such a remarkable athlete was intoxicating; Nashwan had that indefinable presence which so often stamps a champion. One morning, after he had worked on the West Ilsley gallops, his rider turned him to walk back to his stables. Hern watched from his station wagon as the colt's powerful quarters eased him into a fluid stride that a ballet dancer would have envied. 'I can't take my eyes off him; he moves like a panther,' said Hern, rolling his shoulders in imitation of a giant cat.

Similarly, Brian Procter, for twenty years one of Hern's senior work riders, always returns to Nashwan. 'Of all the good horses we have had here, only Nashwan showed at home how good he was. His instant acceleration was unique. The others, and I include the likes of Troy and Henbit, were very lazy. You had to give them a crack down the shoulder to make them concentrate and get on with the job. Nashwan was different: you asked him and he'd quickened and gone in a couple of strides. Even before he'd run I believed he was the best horse we'd had at West Ilsley since Brigadier Gerard.'

Coming from Procter, the image of quiet reflection, that is a remarkable compliment. Brigadier Gerard won seventeen out of eighteen races between 1970 and 1972, including the defeat of Mill Reef in the 1971 2,000 Guineas, and is among the great milers of the century. That Nashwan could even be mentioned in such company suggested that here indeed was something special. Procter's judgement was handsomely vindicated. Nashwan's win in the 2,000 Guineas proved beyond doubt that the colt was more than just a talking horse: he was the genuine article.

In a curious twist of fate, Carson's first involvement with the Nashwan story had been through the colt's dam, Height Of Fashion, whom he had ridden to win the valuable Princess of Wales' Stakes at Newmarket in 1982. Height Of Fashion, a talented filly over middle distances, but short of the highest class, was then owned by the Queen. But her advisers recommended selling the three-year-old and Sheikh Hamdan Al Maktoum, from Dubai, stepped in to buy her for a sum reputedly between £1.4 and £1.8 million.

The sale of Height Of Fashion was the nadir of the royal fortunes, which declined steadily during the eighties. For a variety of reasons the Queen's breeding interests never benefited from the bloodstock boom of the decade. As the bloodstock industry's gravy train pulled out, the royal studs were left on the platform.

These were heady days in the bloodstock business. Yearling prices had risen to lunatic heights on the back of frantic buying by oil-rich Arabs, with the four Al Maktoum brothers, Maktoum, Hamdan, Mohammed and Ahmed, and Prince Khalid Abdullah of Saudi Arabia leading the way. The Maktoums were also buying the best mares as the foundation of their own stud operations, and annexing the finest breeding land in Britain, Ireland and America. This was a new order created almost overnight. Vast oil-based wealth was taking over in an instant the studs and bloodlines which had taken decades to build. During the mid-eighties, Hamdan began to make his presence felt. Sheikh Mohammed had been the first to establish himself in the front rank of owners in Britain; now Hamdan, a deep thinker with a keen racing brain and exhaustive knowledge of horseflesh, was entering the fray in earnest. In Height Of Fashion he saw an ideal brood-mare prospect on which to build his fortunes, and his judgement was impeccable.

It remains an imponderable whether, with greater foresight on the part of her racing advisers, Nashwan would have carried the royal colours. The more pertinent question is, if Height Of Fashion had not been sold, would there even have been a Nashwan? The Queen, despite being the richest woman in the world, has applied only the tiniest fraction of her fortune to her racing interests. Although, during the late seventies, stallions such as Nijinski had been used, by the middle of the following decade the astronomical rise in fees had put the most fashionable North American stallions out of court.

Sheikh Hamdan had no such inhibitions. For Height Of Fashion's first two coverings he chose Northern Dancer, the dominant sire of the seventies and eighties, whose fee had at one time touched $1 million. Her first two foals, Alwasmi and

Unfuwain, were both group race winners in Britain and established her as a producer of high-quality horses. For her third covering, Sheikh Hamdan opted for Blushing Groom, a top-class miler trained in France by François Mathet, but who failed to stay a mile and a half when third to The Minstrel in the 1977 Derby. Blushing Groom, based at Gainesway Farm in Kentucky, had become a sire of international repute with such as Rainbow Quest, the winner of the 1985 Prix de l'Arc de Triomphe to represent him, and was another stallion taken from the top drawer. The result of the mating was Nashwan.

After the Guineas, Nashwan was now a top-priced 2–1 for the Derby, a pleasing prospect for those of us holding fancy odds about his chances there. Carson had no reservations about his qualifications for the world's most important Flat race. 'Nashwan was really digging in at the finish today,' Carson said. 'I've no doubts at all about his stamina and the faster they go in the Derby the happier I will be.'

Hern, too, was confident about Epsom, but reserved his greatest praise for his jockey. 'Willie rode a marvellous race. He just let Nashwan use that long, raking stride. I'm confident he'll get the trip,' he said, referring to the extra half-mile Nashwan would have to cover in the Derby. 'And I'm sure he'll handle the course all right. He could gallop down the side of a house.'

The Nashwan team were in the box seats. They had the proven horse and entertained few fears that either the longer trip or the unique Epsom gradients would prove beyond him. Now it was up to the other trainers to find one to beat Nashwan. The period between the 2,000 Guineas and the Derby is the most exciting time of the Flat racing year. This is the time when the talking has to stop and the horses prove whether or not they have what it takes to be worthy challengers for the Derby. In the spring of 1989 there was only one yardstick for the Classic trials: is the form good enough to beat Nashwan? There were two possible answers in the affirmative, although only one was to have any bearing on Epsom.

At Chester's atmospheric May meeting on the Roodeye, a course so small and sitting so snugly under the ancient city walls that the horses look as though they are on a merry-go-round, Old Vic burst into the public consciousness as a horse bound for the top. A relentless galloper, he pounded the opposition to defeat in the Chester Vase, a race which had re-established itself as a reliable Derby trial in recent years. However, Old Vic's trainer, Henry Cecil, was soon discounting the idea of an Epsom showdown with Nashwan, saying that neither the probable firm ground nor the switchback course would suit his charge. Old Vic would instead go to France, an astute move, as he simply annihilated rivals in the Prix du Jockey-Club, the French Derby, at Chantilly.

Four days after Old Vic's win, another threat emerged, one which would have to be faced at Epsom. Guy Harwood, having been denied the 2,000 Guineas by Nashwan, saddled Cacoethes to win the Derby Trial at Lingfield Park, beating a previous ante-post Derby favourite, Pirate Army, with great authority. Cacoethes, roughly translated from the Greek as 'naughty thoughts', had won himself plenty of admirers with a powerful display on a track noted for its similarity to Epsom. Even Carson had been moved to sit up and take notice. 'It was a good performance,' he conceded. 'He stays well, clearly goes on firm ground and you have to think that he will handle Epsom after winning here.'

A week before the Derby I visited Hern on assignment for *The Times*. I found him sitting at his desk beneath a picture of Carson and Troy, and as I studied the portrait it struck me once more how the most powerful of racehorses are borne by the most fragile of legs. In such a dry summer, as the ground became firmer by the day, it was more than just an idle thought. Hern, as if reading my mind, broke the silence. 'That has been my aim with Nashwan, you know, keeping him sound on the firm going. He was stone fit for the Guineas and my main consideration for the past fortnight has been to keep him ticking over.'

The following day, as usual on work mornings, Carson was waiting in his car for Hern, having driven from his Cirencester home. A red and white quartered cap topped his rider's anorak and breeches as he climbed into Hern's station wagon. Carson was in great form, cheerful, joking, chattering away to Hern. The trainer decided to play up to him. 'That Cauthen,' Hern said. 'What a lovely race he rode yesterday. He really has got a clock in his head.'

Carson rose to the bait. 'You never said anything about that filly I won on the other day, did you?' he said, becoming excitable at the thought of being overlooked. 'I had a clock in my head then.' Hern was waiting. 'Willie,' he said, 'if you had a clock in your head you'd forget to wind it.' Carson laughed. For those around the jockey, one of Nashwan's less publicised virtues had been to restore Carson's sense of humour. When he was on the winning team he could share a joke, even one at his own expense.

The work went well. Nashwan came cruising up the gallops before quickening past his galloping companion as they drew level with us. He was an impressive sight, all smooth athleticism and effortless power. Behind him, back down the gallops, Prince Of Dance thudded along, pounding the ground Nashwan had seemed to glide over.

Each big race brings with it the near-certainty of a scare surrounding the favourite. Nashwan obliged. The Sunday before the Derby, Chantilly racecourse was buzzing, not with news of that day's Prix du Jockey-Club, but with rumours that Nashwan was lame. The pressure for information built so quickly and fiercely that Angus Gold, Sheikh Hamdan's racing manager, was forced to issue a statement. 'Nashwan ripped a shoe off at exercise on Saturday morning,' Gold said. 'Major Hern sent the horse home as a precautionary measure, so he missed his work. However, he had a couple of canters this morning and is absolutely sound again.' And so off we all went to Epsom.

There were twelve runners for the Derby, headed by Nashwan and his principal rival Cacoethes. Hern had also opted to run Prince Of Dance, who would be ridden

Carson and pilot Alan 'Bilko' Biltcliffe with the jockey's private Piper Saratoga – registered G-WILI

by Cauthen, and it was those three who dominated the betting market. Few believed the winner would be found beyond that trio.

Carson had made a habit of driving to Epsom, as he had done before winning on Troy and Henbit. This time he changed his routine. Alan 'Bilko' Biltcliffe, his private pilot, kept Carson's Piper Saratoga Six at an airfield near Oxford. On the morning of the race, Bilko flew to Cirencester, picked up Willie and Elaine, and took them to an airfield south of Epsom. After a helicopter had whisked Carson off to the races, Bilko and Elaine returned to Minster Stud. Apart from a visit to Doncaster to watch Carson ride Minster Son to victory in the St Leger, Elaine had never seen Carson ride a Classic winner in the flesh. She saw no reason to tamper with a successful formula.

As Carson arrived, brimful of confidence, Harwood's spirits were sinking over Cacoethes' chance. Among the first to arrive at Epsom, Harwood went straight out to walk the course to assess how much recent rain had affected the track. Cacoethes loved fast ground, the faster the better, and any softening of the going would be to his disadvantage. Harwood returned to deliver his verdict. 'It's too soft,' he said gloomily. 'It's gone against us.' The betting market was quick to agree. Cacoethes' price slipped out to 3–1 while Nashwan was heavily backed from 9–4 to 5–4. Only Prince Of Dance, at 11–2, offered a realistic alternative to the market leaders.

Derby day is not what it used to be, but even so retains a distinct carnival spirit. Champagne picnics in the car park and top hats and morning dress rub shoulders with fairground rides and gypsies; something for everyone in a year when everyone was preoccupied with one horse: Nashwan.

Nothing looked better than Nashwan in the paddock, nor as he made his way quietly across the Downs to the mile and a half start. From start to finish, the Derby requires jockeyship of the highest quality. Awareness is vital. In the early stages the course turns to the right before the field must edge its way back across to the left for the steep descent down Tattenham Hill and round the course's greatest landmark, Tattenham Corner. Jockeys can be caught badly out of position by the track's unique demands and simply left short of elbow room as others weaken in front of them. The key to the race is usually Tattenham Hill. By this point the race has begun to develop and the likely winner can often be identified. This year it was Nashwan, who was travelling by far the most sweetly. 'When I saw how well he was moving on the hill I knew he would win if he stayed,' Hern said.

Although Cacoethes and Greville Starkey led into the straight, it was only a matter of time before Nashwan asserted his superiority. Just over two furlongs out, Carson sent Nashwan to the front and, in his best punching and driving style, powered Nashwan home five lengths clear of the 500–1 outsider Terimon, who deprived Cacoethes of second in the closing stages.

The cheering quarter of a million crowd had nothing on Bilko, who was going privately mad with a jig of celebration in front of Carson's television. 'But Elaine was doing some washing in the kitchen,' Bilko recalled. 'She was too nervous to watch. The first time she knew we'd won was when I started cheering.'

In the post-race press conference, Hern was in no doubt where Nashwan stood. 'He's the best horse I've trained,' he said. 'Troy wouldn't have had the speed to win the Guineas and I doubt whether as a three-year-old Brigadier Gerard could have won the Derby.' Carson was more guarded. Despite his public image of an inveterate shoot-from-the-hip chatterer, he is often circumspect when it comes to expressing an opinion. He will rarely commit himself, particularly on the merits of horses, until he believes he has enough knowledge to make a sensible judgement. He chose to parry the questions. 'Nashwan could be the best horse I've ridden. He's more versatile than Troy but he still has to prove himself against the older horses. That's the key to his ability.'

At the end of the day, as the crowds drifted away, traffic jammed the roads around the course and litter piled up on the Downs, Carson was taken by helicopter to Fairoaks airfield where he was met by an ecstatic Elaine and Bilko. Having flown back to Cirencester, Carson and Elaine celebrated with a meal at their favourite restaurant, the Bibury Court.

Nashwan's wins in the 2,000 Guineas and the Derby had put him in the position to become the first Triple Crown winner since 1970, if he went on to win the St Leger. That, however, lay in the future as the next step was considered. The King George VI and Queen Elizabeth Diamond Stakes is the premier mid-season meeting between the generations. The Nashwan camp was unanimous in their desire to tackle

*Nashwan has the Derby in safe-keeping
as he powers through Epsom's uphill final furlong*

the Ascot race, but there were divisions on the best route to take. The choice was between the Irish Derby, run over the same mile and a half trip as the Epsom Derby, or the Eclipse Stakes, which is two furlongs shorter and also entails taking on older horses.

To run against older horses over Sandown's ten furlongs is always considered something of a risk. Hern and Carson, with a total of seven Irish Derby wins between them, favoured the more traditional path of going via the Curragh. 'I would certainly prefer to go to Ireland,' Carson said. 'There's more time between that race and Ascot, and also it's a big strain coming back to ten furlongs.' However, the man who pays the piper calls the tune. As usual, Sheikh Hamdan had his own clear opinions, and he wanted to see Nashwan's speed tested against the older generation in the Eclipse. 'Sheikh Hamdan thought that little would be proved by going for the Irish Derby,' Angus Gold said.

Carson's hard-headed approach to his own marketability was evident in the run up to the Eclipse. I approached him to do a preview of the race and he readily agreed – provided the sum of £250 was forthcoming. It was. Having concluded a virtuoso display on the cheque book, Carson then impressed with his grasp of the form book.

On paper, Nashwan was faced with a formidable task against Indian Skimmer and Warning. Indian Skimmer had already shown ten furlongs to be her best distance with wins in the Phoenix and Dubai Champion Stakes the previous season to her name. Warning had been the best miler in Europe the previous season and had shown he retained plenty of his sparkle with an easy win at Royal Ascot the month before the Eclipse.

Carson was ruthless in his assessments. 'It doesn't look as though Warning can possibly stay the trip, either on his breeding or his style of racing,' he said. 'All the rain that's about won't help him either.' So much for his chance. Now Indian Skimmer: 'The soft ground has not come in time for her. Anyway she's not a champion. Henry Cecil [her trainer] got a bit carried away with her last autumn. She's certainly beatable.'

Men of such firm beliefs can often be disastrously wrong in their assessments. But this time Carson was right on the mark, as Indian Skimmer and Warning were well beaten behind Nashwan into third and fourth respectively. Unfortunately for Nashwan, despite his principal opponents running moderately, he was still to have

Nashwan stretches out to win
the 1989 Eclipse Stakes at Sandown

a hard race, which may well have sown the seeds of his later downfall. Opening Verse, ostensibly a pacemaker for Indian Skimmer but a smart, if unpredictable, performer in his own right, set a strong gallop and turned for home eight lengths clear of Nashwan.

Carson, although criticised subsequently for having ridden an over-confident race, was not slow to realise the danger. He swiftly went in pursuit, caught the leader with about a furlong and a half to race and drew away to win by five lengths. Although the win was decisive enough, it had been a fast-run race in demanding conditions and Nashwan appeared to be tiring at the finish. 'I'd wanted to do a Lester Piggott and just win cleverly,' Carson said. 'But eight lengths is a lot to make up on the Sandown hill so I had to go for it.'

All the outward signs, however, showed Nashwan to be none the worse for the race. 'Nashwan trotted out well and was shouting for his grub,' Hern reported the next day. 'He's lost only 4 lb in weight, which is amazing. A horse can lose 10 lb running at Newbury, which is only half an hour away.'

Now Nashwan was set to attempt the unprecedented feat of winning the 2,000 Guineas, Derby, Eclipse and King George in the same season. The signs were

Carson and Nashwan seem to glide to the start for the 1989
King George VI and Queen Elizabeth Diamond Stakes.
'Riding Nashwan is like making love', Carson said

encouraging. He was still sparkling on the gallops and with Cacoethes, comfortably beaten at Epsom, his likely main danger, the opposition did not look severe. The Ascot mile and a half, with its short two and a half furlong home straight, takes some knowing. Discussing tactics before the race, Carson spoke of the dangers of being caught on the hop. 'You have to be awake to the pace of the race, of the way it unfolds,' he said. 'If they've gone slowly you must be within reach of the leaders. If there's been a strong gallop you can come from a long way back, the way I rode Petoski to win the King George.'

The Nashwan camp had taken out some tactical insurance by running Polemos, which, although trained by Tom Jones at Newmarket, was owned by Sheikh Hamdan. Jockey Richard Hills was given the unusual brief of getting to the front and slowing down the gallop in order to maximise Nashwan's speed at the finish. However, the plan lay in ruins as Michael Roberts, riding the outsider Top Class, tried to steal a march by striking for home approaching the straight. Carson, aware that the pace to that point had been slow, kept Nashwan handy and moved up to join the leader early in the straight. A barging match appeared to take place between Top Class and Nashwan before Nashwan wrested the lead.

Then Cacoethes loomed to throw down a challenge. In a spirited duel through the final furlong Nashwan had the deeper resources and prevailed by a neck. It had been his hardest race; never had the winning margin been so small, nor had he ever had to work so grimly for victory. The day was Nashwan's but his mantle of invincibility was gone. He could have been beaten, and Carson, offering a commendably impartial view, believed that he should have been. 'He just wasn't himself today,' he said, 'and if Greville had gone for home earlier we could well have lost.'

While Carson was winning marks for his neutrality in the interpretation of the race, he was at the same time losing them for a display of petulance. Michael Roberts' decision to dash Top Class to the front was universally acknowledged to have been an excellent piece of opportunism, the only chance he had to steal the race on a rank outsider. Top Class may only have been third, but he could not possibly have achieved more. Carson did not subscribe to the general view. 'Roberts rode a terrible race,' snapped Carson. 'Nearly knocked me over, but the stewards did nothing about it.'

Roberts is, without argument, one of the best riders in the world; eleven-times champion in South Africa, associated with some outstanding horses in Britain – including a previous King George winner, Mtoto – always in demand. But critically for Carson, he is one of the few world-class jockeys who is a genuine lightweight. The weight range from 7 st 10 lb to 8 stone, a lucrative hunting ground in the top handicaps and valuable conditions races, had always been Carson's domain. Now, with the arrival of Roberts, he had competition, and did not like it.

After the King George, Nashwan stood on an extraordinarily high pedestal. But, although we had yet to discover the truth for ourselves, we had already seen the best of Nashwan. Neil Graham was among the first to detect the warning signs. 'When

I went to saddle Nashwan at Ascot he was sweating, which he'd never done before. Then he was warm in the paddock. I went to the start with him and he was much more unsettled than usual. He was beginning to lose his punch. I think the racing was beginning to get to him. After all, he'd had three Group One races in a short space of time and by the time Ascot came it had begun to take its toll.' But in the warm glow of triumph there was no place for future fears. Carson, buoyed by the successes of summer, was turning his thoughts to a golden autumn. 'Of course he has to go for the St Leger before the Arc,' he insisted. 'It's the Triple Crown. Any distance, firm or soft, fast-run or slowly run, it's all the same to Nashwan. He's a true champion, the best I've ridden. If he comes back fresh from his rest he'll never be beaten.'

Hern had come to regard Doncaster in September as a personal bailiwick. He had landed the final Classic on six occasions, and was the trainer of Minster Son, the 1988 winner, in all but name. Hern was well aware that his preference for the St Leger might not be shared by Sheikh Hamdan, who was seriously considering missing Doncaster, the better to concentrate on the Arc. Hern, however, continued to beat the drum for the St Leger. 'There are three weeks between the St Leger and the Arc this year,' Hern said. 'The timing has never been better.'

Here was a difference of opinion to intrigue and galvanise the racing press. On the one hand, an admired trainer recently returned to the ranks of public affection; on the other, a fabulously wealthy foreign owner seemingly thumbing his nose at the traditions of the British turf in favour of the Arc. Everyone had an opinion, and few were slow to express them. Tony Morris, a greatly respected observer of racing and its heritage, wrote in the *Racing Post*: 'The Arc has a winner every year; the achievement of a Triple Crown is a once every thirty years event. . . . The sport, the public, and not least Nashwan himself, are all losers as a result of this unadventurous decision.'

But Sheikh Hamdan is a sportsman in the best sense of the word; his desire to concentrate on the Arc was based only on the best interests of Nashwan. 'The Arc was the race Sheikh Hamdan wanted to win above all others,' said Angus Gold. The die was cast. Nashwan would be prepared for the Prix Niel, a recognised Arc trial run at Longchamp three weeks before the big race. I flew to Paris on the morning of the Prix Niel. The city basked in a glorious late summer splendour, the sun blessing the leafy and elegant course. Here was the perfect setting for Nashwan to reaffirm his authority after a near two months rest.

He was relaxed in the parade ring, a little warm, but understandably so on a sultry afternoon. Nor did the early stages of the race give any cause for concern. Nashwan settled well for Carson, tracking the leaders. Turning for home, Pat Eddery struck for home on French Glory. Two furlongs out Carson brought Nashwan to challenge, but as we waited for him to accelerate the unthinkable became reality. He was going to be beaten. For all Carson's urgings Nashwan was apparently standing still, the fire of his greatness extinguished before our eyes. As Nashwan struggled with French

Glory, Golden Pheasant swept past both of them in the final furlong for a clear-cut victory. French Glory was too strong for Nashwan, who was only third.

Carson was disconsolate. 'It's terrible, just terrible,' he muttered as he hauled his saddle back to the weighing room. 'He didn't finish and I can't understand it. He's not even blowing.' Nor could Hern shed any light on the defeat. 'There's no obvious answer,' he said. 'I wouldn't blame the going. He has been working well at West Ilsley and there were no problems travelling. But horses are only flesh and blood.'

Nashwan was none the worse on his return home and tests failed to reveal anything amiss. However, now the plan was changed; he would miss the Arc and go instead for the Dubai Champion Stakes at Newmarket over ten furlongs. The new plan never left the drawing board. Four days before the race a cryptic announcement from West Ilsley stated: 'Nashwan has a temperature of 102 degrees and will be unable to run in the Champion Stakes on Saturday.' In those few, flat words, Nashwan shuffled away. He was retired to his owner's palatial Shadwell Stud near Thetford, Norfolk, to begin stallion duties the following February.

What went wrong on that fateful day at Longchamp? Carson has his theories, but holds them close. 'There was something I can't tell you about because you're the press,' he hinted mysteriously in the days that followed. I believe Nashwan had simply been drained by an arduous campaign. Physically, he had been under pressure all season. Besides the normal demands of the training regime he had been hurried early in the season to bring him along for the 2,000 Guineas. I have no doubts that it left its mark, and returned in the autumn to contribute to his downfall. Graham's view, that he had been losing his edge at Ascot, had come home to roost, all the more spectacularly because Nashwan had been beaten in a race he had been expected to win comfortably. Carson, for all his dark intimations, had, in a separate conversation, virtually subscribed to that view. 'The English Classic programme takes a great deal out of horses,' he said. 'They are knackered by the end of the year. I don't know why, they just are.'

Nashwan's story was to have an astonishing footnote. In the International Classifications, the order of merit, Nashwan was not considered the best three-year-old colt of his year. That accolade was awarded to Old Vic on the strength of his crushing victory in the Prix du Jockey-Club. Although the argument must necessarily be academic, as the two never met, I believe that to consider Old Vic's overall record superior is almost laughable. Nashwan was infinitely the more versatile, as his win in the 2,000 Guineas demonstrated; he was always campaigned in the highest class; and he put older horses to rout in the King George. There is no doubt in my mind he was one of the most exciting horses of the past twenty years.

Measured against Nashwan, the rest of Carson's year all but faded into insignificance. He put together 138 winners, his best total since 1983 when he last won the jockeys' championship. But this was again a year when Eddery and Cauthen dominated the numbers game, with Eddery having the final say.

A pensive Carson:
Willie isn't always the happy-go-lucky, wise-cracking Scot

CHAPTER FIFTEEN

MAJOR DICK HERN

To understand the emotional power of Nashwan's triumphs they need to be seen in the context of Hern's struggle against illness and the move to force his departure from West Ilsley. In March 1989, the magazine *Pacemaker Update* leaked a story that the Queen had decided not to renew Hern's lease on the royal stables when it expired at the end of the year. It also said that William Hastings-Bass, one of the Queen's trainers and a protégé of Lord Carnarvon's, was to be installed as his successor. This rumour had been floated earlier in the year, but never from such an authoritative source.

The press had a field day. Not only was Hern a much respected figure in racing, his courageous fight to cope with disability had fostered a powerful admiration. So, seizing on the issue of 'Queen evicts crippled trainer' (with its undertones of ruthless dismissal after years of faithful service), the press went to town.

Everyone's worst fears were realised on Tuesday 14 March. In an announcement from Buckingham Palace, apparently timed to coincide with the start of the National Hunt meeting at Cheltenham in order to avoid unwelcome publicity, it was announced that the Queen had appointed William Hastings-Bass to take over at her West Ilsley stables when Major Hern's lease expired at the end of the year.

The general attitude was one of stunned disbelief. Not only was Hern obviously in better health, after his holiday in Dubai, than at any time since his accident, his stables, in Prince Of Dance, Nashwan, Al Hareb and Unfuwain, housed as talented a band of colts as had ever been seen in the yard at one time; convincing evidence, if indeed it were needed, of Hern's position as one of the outstanding trainers of the post-war era. Although it was the Queen's right to appoint whom she chose as Hern's successor, Hastings-Bass, a competent and painstaking operator since he began training in 1976, could hardly be considered in the same category as his predecessor.

Not only would Hern have to find elsewhere to train, in pretty quick time at that, in 1990, there was also the question of his loyal staff, most of whom had been with him for years. It was the apparent unfairness of the move that angered people and caused such outspoken criticism from the press. Brough Scott's offering in *The Sunday Times* carried a headline 'Why the Queen is wrong'. It finished by saying 'The Queen's passion for the turf has done this activity untold benefit down the years.

Not surprisingly, racing people have become Royalists to a fault. It is a supreme irony that we may now see them, of all parishes, in revolt.'

Carson reacted to the crisis like a man inspired. Gone were the days of indecision and black depression. 'They made a bad decision,' he thundered. 'I've nothing against Hastings-Bass, but there's no way he's going to fill the yard like Major Hern did. He'll be a hard act to follow. There could be a lot of people out of work in the village. It's an upheaval. That's the truth, and no one can get at you for speaking the truth. The Major has come a long way through a very dark tunnel since his accident and now, just when we were beginning to see the light, it's as though someone had dropped a trapdoor and shut off that light.' On a personal note, he added, 'It's certainly put my future in jeopardy. If the Major can't find a yard I'll retire. I certainly wouldn't go on without a top job.'

The seeds of action in these matters were, of course, sown some time previously, and the catalyst for the apparently insensitive decision had been Hern's heart operation in June. Since then, events had moved forward with the inevitability of a Greek tragedy. The principal actors in the drama were Lord Carnarvon on the one hand and Sheilah Hern on the other. Both are strong willed to the point of intolerance. When it came to protecting her crippled husband's interests and livelihood, Sheilah was to prove as a tigress defending an injured cub. In July, after Nashwan had won the Derby, I stood on the downs with Mrs Hern watching Nashwan circling the Major. 'All last year when Dick was so ill, I felt that this horse was trying to tell us something. I was determined that whatever happened Dick was to be up here training the horse again this season.'

It is impossible to be certain what happened during those difficult months. Neither side has ever discussed the matter, Buckingham Palace never feeling it necessary to justify its actions and both the Herns being traditionally as close-mouthed as oysters. But, having talked to various interested people at the time and since, it is possible to have some understanding of what must have occurred. An owner in the stable told me: 'It must be understood that the owners of the stable were very worried about the future. The doctors had told them that Major Hern's future was uncertain and there was so much to consider. For example, there were the other owners in the yard. They wanted to know about what was going to happen, as they would be having yearlings to place in the autumn. Remember that at that time it was thought that the responsibility of training would kill him, not the reverse.'

What no one could have foreseen was that Hern was going to make rapid improvement physically. 'Things suddenly changed,' said an owner. 'Everybody for the first time realised what would happen if Dick had to give up, that it might kill him. He became very demoralised at the idea. And Sheilah was pushing harder and harder to get everything changed. Then of course he went to Dubai and came back in even better health. But by then the chain of events was in motion and it was too late to stop.'

After the Queen's announcement had been made in March, the public resentment continued to mount. And of course everyone had a chance to show their feelings when Nashwan won the 2,000 Guineas. All this time, behind the scenes, desperate attempts were being made to find a solution. 'First it was suggested that he should become racing manager to Lady Beaverbrook, but that idea didn't appeal at all,' said the owner. 'They even offered to build new stables in the paddocks on the right-hand side going down to the yard. Dick was quite in favour, but Sheilah was dead against it. She was right; I don't think it would have worked.' Finally, a compromise solution was reached when it was announced at the York spring meeting that Hern was to be allowed to share the training facilities with Hastings-Bass for the 1990 season.

Carson, who had landed a 76–1 treble at York on the afternoon of the announcement, greeted the news with reservations. 'This is marvellous news for the Major and his staff, as there will once again be a comfortable atmosphere in the village. But I'm still not sure whether I will go on riding next season. Opportunities may become more limited and everything is still up in the air.'

Later that year it was announced that Sheikh Hamdan Al Maktoum was prepared to build new stables for the man who had given him so much pleasure and profit with Nashwan. After a prolonged search, it was decided to purchase Kingwood House from Mark Smyly. Millions of pounds were spent on buildings and gallops. And, of course, to show his gratitude further, the Sheikh gave Willie a contract to ride the pick of his total of around 300 horses in training in Britain. How well was Carson to repay that trust.

Carson (centre) on the gallops at West Ilsley

Willie easily winning the Fred Darling Stakes
at Newbury on Salsabil in 1990

CHAPTER SIXTEEN
GOLDEN DAYS

If the year of Nashwan had seen the complete revival of Carson's fortunes, 1990 represented the year of magnificent consolidation. Here he was, approaching his forty-eighth birthday, yet apparently defying time. The statistics supported what our eyes and the form book told us: that he was riding better than ever.

During the winter, Carson had signed a contract which made him first jockey to Sheikh Hamdan Al Maktoum, the finance minister of oil-rich Dubai. Sheikh Hamdan, together with his brother, Sheikh Mohammed, and Prince Khalid Abdullah of Saudi Arabia, were the great triumvirate in whose hands the power of European racing lay. The contract represented the security which Willie craved. When Pat Eddery signed to ride for Abdullah several years previously, rumour suggested that Eddery's price was in the region of £2 million for a three-year contract. Carson, never shy when it came to his own worth, would have had that figure in mind as a guideline.

The quality which the Arabs respect above all others is loyalty. Sheikh Hamdan was impressed not only by Carson's handling of Nashwan, but by his outspoken support of Dick Hern throughout the trainer's difficulties. Those events – his accident and the controversy surrounding his tenure at West Ilsley – had also contrived to reduce his string numerically. Simply, Carson had fewer horses to ride. 'It was a logical development,' says Angus Gold, Sheikh Hamdan's racing manager. 'Willie needed a wider range of opportunities.'

Carson now had the pick of the Sheikh's horses with a wide range of trainers, and there was plenty to look forward to on the Classic front. At West Ilsley, Hern had Elmaamul and Nashwan's half-brother, Mukddaam, as big-race hopefuls; Peter Walwyn was relying on Rami; and, best of all, John Dunlop had the filly Salsabil. Salsabil's two-year-old career, concluded with a victory in the Prix Marcel Boussac at Longchamp, France's premier race for juvenile fillies, had been sufficient to have her installed as winter favourite for the 1,000 Guineas.

Despite Carson's association with the Dunlop stable, which stretched back some twenty years, he had never ridden an English Classic winner for the stable. In all other respects their professional relationship had been astonishingly successful. By the end of 1990 they had shared a total of 451 winners, compared with Eddery's score for the stable of 121 and Piggott's 63. They had also collected twenty wins

Carson narrowly wins the 1,000 Guineas
at Newmarket on Salsabil from Heart Of Joy

in Group One races, the highest echelon of European racing. But that missing Classic was nagging at Carson and he wanted to put right the omission.

Salsabil's first race in 1990 was in the Fred Darling Stakes at Newbury. She was breathtakingly impressive. Carson squeezed her through a narrow gap to give her room to race, and she responded with an explosive burst of acceleration to come home six lengths clear of Haunting Beauty. The bookmakers' first offer of 3–1 for the 1,000 Guineas disappeared in the twinkling of an eye. After the dust had settled, 6–4 was the best price to be had anywhere. Nor could Carson find any fault with Salsabil. 'That was highly satisfactory,' he said. 'If she can repeat that performance on 1,000 Guineas day she'll be very hard to beat.'

While Salsabil's reputation went from strength to strength, the same could not be said for Carson's possible mounts in the 2,000 Guineas. Although Elmaamul and Mukddaam had won their respective reappearances, neither had shown enough to suggest ready-made Classic quality. For the moment, though, Salsabil was enough to satisfy even the most demanding jockey's Classic appetite. On 1,000 Guineas day Salsabil started a firm 6–4 favourite with Heart Of Joy, the winner of the Nell Gwyn Stakes at Newmarket, second best at 4–1. The betting had the race weighed up to perfection. After a fierce struggle through the last two furlongs, Carson drove Salsabil ahead to win by half a length from Heart Of Joy. It was his first success in the 1,000 Guineas, the only Classic which had eluded him. 'Salsabil hated the firm ground today,' was Carson's immediate reaction. 'She had to dig deep into her reserves to win. I picked the right horse to track in Heart Of Joy and she was going better than Salsabil until the last half furlong.'

The usual guessing game about a Classic winner's next engagement was soon in full swing. Rather than have time to savour Salsabil's triumph, Dunlop and Carson were soon being prompted by the press to reveal her next objective. The key issue was stamina. Her sire, Sadler's Wells, had not won beyond ten furlongs, but had proved capable of siring top-class winners over longer distances. However, her dam,

With Salsabil after her 1,000 Guineas triumph

Flame Of Tara, showed her best form at a mile and did not look an influence for stamina. It was no easy decision.

Carson was keenly aware of how much stamina was required to win the Oaks over an extra half mile. His three previous winners of the race, Dunfermline, Bireme and Sun Princess, had all been thorough stayers. Still wearing the blue and white colours he had carried to victory, Carson weighed the alternatives. 'A mile and a quarter, yes, she will definitely stay,' he said. 'But a mile and a half? You couldn't be certain.'

Carson's chances of completing a double in the 2,000 Guineas were slim. Given the choice of Elmaamul and Rami he opted for Elmaamul, but he was never in with a serious chance as Tirol held off the French challenger Machiavellian. Curiously, his retainer with Sheikh Hamdan, having provided one Classic, probably deprived him of another. Tirol's trainer, Richard Hannon, employed Carson on a regular basis and they had shared the 2,000 Guineas three years earlier with Don't Forget Me. Elmaamul finished seventh after meeting some interference. 'It certainly didn't cost us a winning chance,' Carson said. 'He may have finished fourth or fifth, but really he will be much better suited by further than a mile.'

The Salsabil debate was swiftly resolved. Against the advice of trainer and jockey, Sheikh Hamdan came down in favour of aiming Salsabil at the Oaks. Epsom would be her next outing. 'I think he felt that the filly had already proved her point over a mile,' said Angus Gold. 'And he badly wanted to win the Oaks.' That was the question of Carson's Oaks ride solved, but the Derby picture was looking rather bleaker. Elmaamul was his prime candidate, but there were doubts about his best trip. Carson had already expressed an opinion that he would be better over further than a mile; now it had to be established whether a mile and a half was his trip. Hern sent him for the Predominate Stakes over ten furlongs at Goodwood in an attempt to unearth some clue. He ran respectably, finishing four lengths second to Razeen, trained by Henry Cecil, after being hampered in running. Yet it was a performance still some way short of Classic standard. In the run-up to the Derby, Elmaamul worked well in blinkers, satisfying even as severe a judge as Carson. 'He went pretty well,' he admitted. 'He could be all right.'

From Elmaamul's first win of the season Carson had insisted that the colt had been playing around. Now his astute judgement of horses was being vindicated. However, even in an only average year, Carson would go to the Derby with no obvious chance of following up Nashwan's triumph of the previous year. Come Derby day, Linamix and Zoman, the first and second in the French 2,000 Guineas, Quest For Fame, runner-up in the Chester Vase, and Razeen vied for public attention. Elmaamul had faded to the fringes of the argument.

Eddery and Quest For Fame were always travelling well, although Carson's hopes were rising two furlongs from home as Elmaamul looked the only danger. But Quest For Fame was to run on strongly to win by three lengths from the fast-finishing Blue Stag, who deprived Elmaamul of second. Carson and Hern were delighted with

Salsabil easily wins the 1990 Oaks at Epsom

the running of Elmaamul, who was now beginning to fulfil his potential. 'If he'd stayed the mile and a half we would definitely have finished second,' Carson said. Elmaamul was showing himself to be a mile and a quarter horse.

Attention now switched to the Oaks and Salsabil. I took an even greater interest than usual in the Oaks as, having selected the winners of the first three Classics, I was keen to maintain the sequence. As the rain fell, particularly heavily on Thursday evening, I became indecisive, fearing for Salsabil's stamina on the softened ground. Kartajana, in contrast, was believed to favour easy going. In desperation I rang Carson on his car phone. 'Why not stick with a Classic-winning filly?' was his line of reasoning. 'She likes soft going and I'm sure she'll stay the trip.' I ignored his advice and was soon regretting it. Kartajana sweated away her chance in the long preliminaries and was finished before the race had begun. Carson, true to his word – that he thought Salsabil would stay – rode her accordingly. He sent her to the front two furlongs out and she stormed clear to beat Game Plan by five lengths. Kartajana was last of the eight runners.

Carson was in excellent fettle after the race. 'She is the most brilliant of my Oaks winners,' he said. 'She has so many changes of gear.' Salsabil's victory was also a tribute to the growing reputation of Sheikh Hamdan as a judge of his horses. He had insisted that the Oaks was the right race for Salsabil and had been majestically proved correct. 'Sadler's Wells was second in the French Derby on soft ground and also second in the King George,' said the Sheikh, underlining Sadler's Wells' form over a mile and a half. 'And there's plenty of stamina on the dam's side as well.'

After Epsom, the racing world's thoughts turn towards Royal Ascot with its pageantry, high living and spectacular fashion. Just as the fans look forward to the excitement of the great occasion, so do jockeys crave the intoxicating sensation of speed and power that comes from riding high-class thoroughbreds at the season's top meeting. 'My motivation's very basic: I love good horses and riding them is what I do best,' Carson once said. Willie was looking forward to riding Dayjur, also owned by Sheikh Hamdan, at Ascot. A useful two-year-old, Dayjur had shown Willie just a glimpse of something special when winning at Nottingham. Marcus Tregoning, Hern's assistant, remembers the occasion well. 'He jumped out and made all the running. Willie picked him up and he showed tremendous speed for a few seconds.' The rising young star also had a marvellous temperament. 'Willie was always delighted to sit on him. He was so laid back, which is unusual in a sprinter,' says Tregoning.

The key to understanding Dayjur was found after an unsuccessful attempt to restrain the three-year-old went awry in a comparatively minor event over six furlongs at Newbury in May. Sent off favourite, he was eventually beaten a head by the northern challenger Tod. 'It was a great mistake to have him held up,' says Hern. 'After that we decided to let him bowl along as he liked.' He showed his appreciation of this when bolting home by two lengths from the favourite, Statoblest, in the Temple Stakes at the Sandown Whitsun Holiday meeting. 'It came as a complete surprise to Willie,' says Mike Cattermole, Carson's agent.

Both Willie and Sheikh Hamdan went to Ascot breathing fire and thunder. Even after the magnificent start to the campaign, the best times still appeared to lie ahead. But the jockey had a slightly disappointing meeting. Cauthen and Eddery shared the honours with five winners apiece, but Willie only managed a couple, scoring on Hateel and Dayjur for the Sheikh. Dayjur once again put up an impressive performance when storming home by two and a half lengths from the crack French sprinter, Ron's Victory, in the King's Stand Stakes. However, the fact that Dayjur was in the line-up at all on the rain-softened ground was entirely due to the owner's

Dayjur sprints away with the King's Stand Stakes
at Royal Ascot in 1990

insistence that his budding champion should be allowed to take his chance. Both Carson and Hern had been full of forebodings. 'I was convinced that Dayjur was only effective on firm ground and wanted to withdraw him,' said the trainer, 'but Sheikh Hamdan was definite that he wanted the horse to run.'

Once again Sheikh Hamdan's knowledge of equine matters had come up trumps. During the meeting, Dunlop had been harassed by the media for a decision about Salsabil's next race. 'Sheikh Hamdan kept on putting the decision off,' remembers Dunlop, 'and it was only on the Saturday when we were walking towards the saddling boxes to get Shadayid ready for her race that he turned to me and said "The Eclipse or the Irish Derby, it's your decision". I told him then and there that I wanted to go to the Curragh.'

Two factors had swayed the trainer into taking on the colts in the Irish Classic in preference to tackling the older horses in the ten-furlong Eclipse Stakes. The first had been a cable from John Magnier, Vincent O'Brien's son-in-law and the boss of the Coolmore Stud. 'It read: "Well done, what about the Irish Derby?",' says the trainer. 'Before that I had had a long talk with Jim Bolger, who trained Flame

155

Of Tara, Salsabil's dam. He was absolutely convinced that she had stayed a mile and a half well. And after all it was only logical to avoid taking on her elders at this early stage of the season.'

Irresistibly carried along by the momentum of his own success, Carson was about to embark on one of the most remarkable weeks of his energetic career. By the time he arrived at Newcastle on the Saturday of the Irish Derby weekend, his tally was already thirteen victories in five days. The Saturday proved to be simply sensational. By the close of play, the jockey had not only won the big race, the Northumberland Plate, on Al Maheb, he had booted home another five winners, making it a six-timer of 3,266–1. In the process he became only the third man after Sir Gordon Richards and Alec Russell, to ride that number of winners in an afternoon. He had also ridden eighty-four winners, nearly double his total at the same time in the previous season.

Salsabil wins the 1990 Irish Derby from Deploy

The pace at which Carson lives his crowded life is, I find, almost unbelievable. By Sunday morning, the jockey, disdaining the scheduled airlines in favour of his Piper Saratoga – registration G-WILI – was battling his way against strong headwinds across Wales and the Irish Sea for his date with destiny with Salsabil. The adverse weather almost took its toll: Carson arrived at the course only just in time.

Surprisingly, the Irish Derby proved to be little more than a formality for Salsabil. Quest For Fame, the Derby winner, started favourite at 5–4, but was struggling early in the straight and finished a well-beaten fourth. Lengthening her stride magnificently entering the last furlong, Salsabil won by three-quarters of a length from the outsider Deploy, and in the process became the only filly to land the treble of the 1,000 Guineas, the Oaks and the Irish Derby. For good measure, Dunlop and Carson made it a double for the British visitors when also winning the Railway Stakes with Time Gentlemen.

The remorseless Carson was up and running again the next day when he flew to Wolverhampton to ride another four winners. He had now had seventeen winners in four days.

One of the secrets of his seemingly relentless energy is the superb way in which he has organised his life from his Minster Stud in Gloucestershire. Everything is subordinated towards producing him fit and relaxed at the races. Carson bought Minster Stud in 1980 when it was known as Ampney Stud. He has increased the stud from sixty acres to around 150, turning it into a showpiece establishment. Apart from a palatial main house, the stud has two cottages, one occupied by the stud groom and one regularly used by Carson's parents, Tommy and May. His eight mares include Minster Son's dam Honey Bridge. It has become one of the great pleasures of his life. 'I only wish I'd done it earlier,' he said. 'I drive a tractor, mend fences, I'm a jack of all trades. I must enjoy it because I'm often out until eight or nine working.'

Mike Cattermole, an important cog in the machine, is in daily contact. 'Tuesdays and Saturdays he rides work at West Ilsley. He drives over from Cirencester, but is still back home about 10 a.m. He goes straight down to the stud to check out the horses. After that he gives me a ring about 11.00 or 11.30 so I can update him on his rides.'

The jockey usually takes a bath or shower before driving to the airstrip to meet his pilot Alan 'Bilko' Biltcliffe prior to flying high above Britain's crowded motorways to the races. 'He always wears a shirt and tie and makes sure he is well groomed and always looks smart without being a snappy dresser.'

Even when there is no evening meeting, the jockey feels little inclination for socialising. 'He seldom takes Elaine out to dinner. He likes to sit down and watch his satellite television. He's got about fifty channels. He expects Elaine to give him a drink followed by dinner on his lap. He just sits there recharging his batteries.' 'Television is my meditation,' Carson has admitted. 'I like to wind down, have a scotch, watch television until the dot comes. Of course, nowadays it never does.'

Next day, the cycle begins again. 'He's usually at his perkiest in the mornings, but you never know what sort of mood he's going to be in when you ring him,' Cattermole says. 'He could have ridden a treble the day before and be down, or he could have gone two or three days without a winner and still be joking and laughing. You never know how he is going to be, he's very, very unpredictable.'

Nothing succeeds like success, and the Carson luck continued the next weekend. Creator, the 6–5 favourite for the Coral Eclipse Stakes, sulked at the rear of the field as Carson drove Elmaamul past the post half a length in front of Terimon.

Willie and Elaine
relax at home

Although he was fortunate to find Creator out of form, Carson was riding with the irresistible timing of a world-class athlete at his peak. He had now harvested thirty-one winners in a fortnight and ninety-four during the season – and we were still only at the beginning of July. His judgement had once again been vindicated. 'I said at the time that if Elmaamul had stayed, he would have finished second in the Derby,' he said. 'It looks as if I was right.'

The Newmarket July meeting yielded five more winners, the most important victory being gained on Mujtahid for Sheikh Hamdan in the July Stakes. By the Thursday evening, the final day of the meeting, he was only ten behind Eddery in the race for the jockeys' championship. Although the jockey himself never took it seriously, the bookmakers were now offering only 3–1 against the Scot clinching the title for the sixth time.

It was not all plain sailing. Friday began with a visit to Warwick where his only ride ended in defeat on Blue Tail. He then flew on to York where four mounts yielded a solitary success on Jimmy Barnie for Dunlop. Finally, there came a hop across the Pennines to Chester for three more lost causes. In all, he had had eight mounts and been on six beaten favourites.

Sadly, Salsabil missed her next planned engagement: the King George at Ascot. All Carson received for riding the outsider Husyan into a well-beaten eighth place was a telling-off from Peter Walwyn for having ridden an injudicious race. For once, Sheikh Hamdan may have made an error of judgement in not allowing Salsabil to take her chance because of the firm ground. 'It was all very difficult, as Willie had been adamant that the firm ground at Newmarket hadn't suited her at all,' Dunlop says. 'Sheikh Hamdan took considerable account of that. Nicky Beaumont, the clerk of the course at Ascot, had done a marvellous job of watering and there was no sting in the ground. But the owner still decided against running. He was only thinking of the filly. I'm sure there was no question of avoiding Belmez and Old Vic.' The result was a triumph, not only for Henry Cecil, but also for Sheikh Mohammed, as Belmez and Old Vic, both owned by him, fought out a dramatic finish.

Now the delights of Goodwood and York's Ebor meeting lay in store. Carson rode four winners at the Sussex summer festival, but for the first time for years Dick Hern failed to land a blow at the meeting. To say that Carson took York by storm would be no overstatement. He had a flurry of seven winners during the three days and won the Ritz Club Trophy awarded to the leading rider at the meeting. In the Juddmonte International Stakes, Elmaamul ran well to finish second, but failed to match the finishing speed of the remarkable but inconsistent In The Groove. His four winners on the first two days included Hellenic in the Yorkshire Oaks, and Mujtahid in the Gimcrack Stakes. On the Thursday he landed a 28–1 treble on Jallad, Dayjur and Comstock.

Dayjur's sparkling exhibition of controlled power as the 4–6 favourite shattered the five-furlong track record by 1.08 seconds in the Nunthorpe Stakes drew

Carson drives out Elmaamul to beat Terimon
in the Eclipse Stakes at Sandown in 1990

spontaneous tribute from the professionals. It was only then, for the first time, that we realised that Hern's three-year-old might prove to be one of the outstanding sprinters of the century.

On the first Sunday in September, Carson was the darling of the Dublin crowds packed into Phoenix Park as he drove Elmaamul, a heavily backed favourite at 2–1, to a one and a half length victory in the last running of the Phoenix Champion Stakes – the course was closed at the end of the season. Once again, the Carson luck held good as Saumarez, later to win the Arc, ran inexplicably badly and finished seventh of the eight runners.

At Haydock the following Saturday, Dayjur once again was awarded all the accolades after winning the Ladbroke Sprint Cup. Gaining his first important success over six furlongs, the 1–2 favourite showed no signs of stopping in the final two hundred yards.

Carson had little chance of adding to his Classic haul with his last opportunity, the St Leger. He partnered Rubicund for John Dunlop, but the 16–1 outsider rarely held out much hope of success, finishing a comfortably held fourth to Snurge.

The St Leger over, there was a concerted rush to Longchamp for the important Arc trials. Carson was due to ride Salsabil in one of them, the Prix Vermeille, France's top race for fillies. Carson excelled himself. The race was run at a crawl in the early stages and Carson made an inspired move when dashing Salsabil into a decisive lead one and a half furlongs from home. Miss Alleged came with a rattle to be only a neck behind at the line, with the fast finishing In The Groove only half a length away in third.

Although there were doubts about the value of the form because of the false gallop, Salsabil was extending her enviable habit of winning. Connections were fully satisfied. 'I'm looking forward to riding her in the Arc,' said Carson. 'I've been there with plenty of good chances in the past on Troy, Ela-Mana-Mou and Sun Princess. But I feel that Salsabil is outstanding.' Dunlop was a proud man as he welcomed Sheikh Hamdan's filly back to the unsaddling enclosure after recording the fifth win of her career. 'She's only been back in serious work for three weeks after her rest. She's only done four pieces of work and I'm sure she will improve 10 lb on that.'

On Arc day, the first Sunday in October, 12,000 British visitors descended on Longchamp with high hopes of sweeping the board. Earlier in the day they were given plenty to shout about when Zoman, Dayjur and Shadayid were all British-trained winners. Dayjur and Shadayid were both ridden by Carson. In the Prix de l'Abbaye, Dayjur proved himself to be one of the outstanding champion sprinters of all time when bursting five lengths clear of his rivals at half-way. There was a moment of panic when the 1–10 favourite was distracted by a shadow but he still beat Lugana Beach by two lengths. Bearing in mind the disaster that was lurking round the corner for Carson and Dayjur in the Breeders' Cup at Belmont Park, the incident close to home was highly significant. 'About half a furlong from home there is a big tower and Dayjur saw its shadow and jumped it,' said Carson, 'and after that his concentration was shocking and he was reading the signs on the board.'

Hopes were therefore high when Willie rode out on Salsabil for the Arc. But not for nothing is the gruelling Paris test known as the world's most demanding Flat race. Salsabil was installed a short-priced favourite to end her hitherto unbeaten campaign on a further note of glory. But the filly was always struggling and could only finish tenth behind Saumarez. 'I thought things had worked out well and I got myself into a good position. Coming into the turn she was going reasonably well, but suddenly ran out of petrol,' said Carson.

Salsabil was retired after her Arc defeat, leaving Carson to ride Elmaamul in the Champion Stakes at Newmarket. But the three-year-old had had a tough and busy season. To the fury of Salsabil's supporters, the official handicapper made In The Groove 1 lb the better filly. Judged on the result of the Champion Stakes alone, this rating may have been justified. But Salsabil, in winning three Classics and another Group One race, the Prix Vermeille, in her second season had In The Groove behind her on three occasions.

Dayjur wins the Prix de l'Abbaye at Longchamp in 1990.
But his jump near the finishing line foreshadowed
his bizarre defeat in the Breeders' Cup later in the month

Willie wearing the silks of Hamdan Al Maktoum,
whose horses, including Dayjur and Salsabil,
made 1990 such a memorable year for Carson.

CHAPTER SEVENTEEN
DAYJUR·

With the great races of Europe behind us for another year, the sport's circus crossed the Atlantic for the seventh running of the Breeders' Cup series. For aficionados, the Breeders' Cup represents the most exciting show on earth. I have watched dawn break over the San Gabriel mountains behind Santa Anita racecourse in suburban Los Angeles, at Hollywood Park, at the historic Churchill Downs in Kentucky and at Gulfstream Park, Florida. But nowhere was the atmosphere of the build-up more compelling than it was at the Long Island track.

Dayjur, fresh from his triumph in the Prix de l'Abbaye, was one of the spearheads for the strongest European attack yet launched on what was becoming the world championship of racing. British, French and Irish raiders are always at a tremendous disadvantage. Apart from the demands of transatlantic travel, they must race on sharp circuits in unfamiliar surroundings. Highlighting the problem, D. Wayne Lukas, the record stakes earning trainer of all time said, 'Europeans have so much to overcome. Although horses from California have to travel just as far to New York, everything else is much the same. For our horses, the barn areas, the track conditions and the training are all very similar. The Europeans face new conditions and horses are very much creatures of habit.'

However, despite all the drawbacks, the lure of the ten million dollar prize money, the excitement and the prestige still beckons irresistibly to the Europeans. In 1990, apart from Dayjur, Royal Academy, with the amazing 54-year-old Lester Piggott in the saddle, Saumarez, the Arc winner, Priolo and Cacoethes were also star attractions.

The build-up to this extravaganza of racing is a reporter's dream. Training takes place in the full glare of publicity. Lukas and Charlie Whittingham, the legendary 'bald eagle' are among the professionals holding court to the media in their respective barns. This was a clarion call to battle to Hern, a hardened veteran of so many campaigns. At a full-scale press conference, organised in Tommy Skiffington's barn, where Dayjur was stabled, he confronted batteries of reporters and photographers, patiently answering hundreds of questions. 'It will be difficult to win and I am under no illusions,' he said. 'We are taking on the local experts under conditions which will suit them and not us. But Dayjur is by far and away the fastest horse I've ever trained. This is my best chance of ever winning a Breeders' Cup event.'

Before the arrival of the Dayjur team, all the media, both American and British, had been busy giving the thumbs down to Dayjur's chances. American sprinters racing on dirt are blisteringly fast into their stride and previous efforts by European-trained speed specialists had been disastrous. To make things worse, Dayjur had been drawn at thirteen, one from the outside. The visitors were even more despondent, but not so Dayjur's host trainer, Skiffington. 'I think it will help. There's no way Dayjur can lead all the way. Our sprinters are incredibly quick breakers and if Dayjur takes them on, he will have nothing left for the finish. These sprints are like rugby matches with a lot of jostling and barging. Willie's draw at thirteen gives him a chance of being able to settle down and ride a waiting race.'

British hopes were raised dramatically on the Friday morning. Carson, wearing a white mackintosh jacket and an orange and white quartered cap, came out on the track to ride Dayjur in a spin with one of Skiffington's horses. The pair started to increase pace after a furlong and Dayjur quickened impressively to go clear after rounding the bend. This performance galvanised local work watchers. In a land where time is king, Dayjur's performance had been breathtaking. He had returned 45.3 seconds for four furlongs, fully a second faster than any of the other fifty horses to have worked that morning. Gallops are not the real thing of course, but the time had certainly inspired confidence that Dayjur would be able to handle the dirt track.

The nerve centre of activity after the work was the hustle, bustle and warmth of Liz's Kitchen café in the back stretch. High on adrenalin, Carson was cheerfully tucking into fried eggs and crispy bacon. 'Before today I was a bit concerned how he would handle the surface,' he said. 'I'm a lot more confident now but I still feel a bit like Neil Armstrong, setting foot on the moon for the first time.' Carson's confidence had been echoed the night before by Brian Procter, who had flown over from Britain with the horse. 'He's the most laid-back horse I've ever known. He loved the flight and never took his head out of his hay net. He's enjoyed everything over here, even having a day off. I think he'll win.'

Never have so many experts, both European and American, been so wrong in their pre-race calculations. Only one of the most bizarre incidents in racing history cost Dayjur the first prize. With the race at his mercy the horse jumped a shadow only strides from the finishing line to present the prize to Safely Kept. The memory is unforgettable. The bright October sun had cast a shadow of the timer's booth right across the course, and there was another shadow on the finishing line. Thirty minutes later the shadows had moved on.

The sight of Dick Francis among the 66,000 spectators was a forcible reminder of how much the accident to Dayjur resembled that astonishing moment in 1956, when the jockey on the Queen Mother's Devon Loch all but won the Grand National, when the horse collapsed on the run-in and was passed by ESB.

'I just can't believe it,' said a bewildered Carson. 'He jumped a shadow and then

jumped another on the line. I was going to win by a length, but we got beat. He had done a similar thing when winning the Prix de l'Abbaye.' Weeks of careful planning by Hern and brilliant jockeyship by Carson had been set at nought by this freak accident. But in view of the fact that a similar incident had occurred in Paris, it set some observers wondering why a sheepskin noseband or some other aid to concentration had not been used. Answering this criticism Hern said, 'I never thought there would be any shadows, and I don't suppose it would have made any difference anyway. It was just one of those things. It was a day of drama wasn't it? A day we will remember all our lives.'

When interviewed, Carson, reflecting on Dayjur's outstanding record in Europe, struck a philosophical note. 'We may have been beaten. We may not have won the money, but we've still got the best horse.' The jockey's sporting attitude was not appreciated by an agonised Brooklyn punter. 'What an asshole,' his voice boomed from the crowd. In New York winning is the name of the game.

In reality, the jockey had been hard hit. Alan Biltcliffe, the jockey's pilot, said later, 'Normally Willie is amazingly relaxed. He takes adversity very well. I've only seen him het up and agonised once or twice in the twenty years I've known him. Dayjur getting beat in New York was one of those occasions.'

Traumatic as the afternoon had been for Carson, nothing could spoil the most successful season the jockey had ever known. Continuing on the winning trail back home in Britain, he finished the season with a personal best of 187 winners. He passed another milestone in August when he joined Doug Smith in third place in the all-time jockeys list when partnering Joud to victory in the Blue Peter Stakes at Newmarket. The Dancing Brave filly was Carson's 3,112th career winner. In going clear of Doug Smith the following afternoon when winning the Tattersalls Tiffany Highflyer Stakes on Flying Brave, Carson was taking over from the man he had replaced as first jockey to Lord Derby so many years before. In the all-time list of British greats, Carson is now third behind Sir Gordon Richards and Lester Piggott.

Even allowing for the disappointment of Dayjur in the Breeders' Cup, Carson could look back on a season which, nine months earlier, he would hardly have dared dream about. His final total of 187 winners was a remarkable performance, which in most years would have been enough to secure him a sixth jockeys' championship. This particular year, however, was different. Pat Eddery took the title, but it needed a double-century for him to do it, the first since Sir Gordon Richards, thirty-eight years earlier.

Carson indeed basked in the warmth of his retainer, but was not always keen that others should share his success, even those who might have advanced a strong case. Mike Cattermole, who has booked Carson's rides since the start of the 1989 season, recalls. 'Willie had a dream season in 1990, winning a whole host of big races for his retainer and for outside stables. Naturally, there are instances when a big-race ride falls into your lap. But there are other occasions when you get hold of a ride as a result of your own initiative.

'I find that very satisfying in itself, though I can't recall Willie offering his thanks after I have found him a good winner. But he is the first to have a go if you have got it wrong! During 1990, he had more than 120 outside winners, including the Racecall Gold Trophy at Redcar, the Cesarewitch, plus a six-timer at Newcastle. But, though I know him well enough to know he was delighted about all this, it simply isn't in his nature to show it. Willie will always remember if somebody has let him down in the past. It is amazing the things he does remember. But, although he can be fiercely defensive about himself, he can also be a staunch ally — immensely loyal. He once told me that he would ride through fire for Dick Hern and I believe him.'

Carson once revealed his stark philosophy. 'There are only two things which frighten me,' he said. 'Death and ending up skint.' None of us can do much about the former, but Carson has always given the impression of making sure the latter never happens. He has never thrown off the cloak of the early years, when times were hard and money had to be stretched down to the last penny. Carole, his first wife, recalls his 'deep-rooted Scottish thriftiness'. She adds: 'He was always careful. A lot of stable lads have told me that even now he is not the most generous of people. He doesn't give much to anyone when he has a big winner. Whatever Willie is doing you can always rely on him to get the most out of it for himself.'

Ironically, Carson's reluctance to spend more than he believed absolutely necessary has probably cost him even greater wealth. He eschewed the use of a business agent, preferring instead to make deals himself. Requests for interviews would be greeted with a price and a justification. 'I've only got so long to go,' he once bellowed down the telephone at me. 'I'm entitled to make as much out of it while I can.'

Yet he has often undersold himself. He is one of the rare jockeys to have reached the public's heart, to have bridged the gap between sport and popular appeal. On television he appeared as a team captain on the BBC's *A Question of Sport* and as a panellist on the game show *Celebrity Squares*. It was Carson to whom the *Racing Post* newspaper turned to advertise its launch. How many of his colleagues can rival his high media profile? As Carson once said to me, 'If Pat Eddery and I were walking down the street, people would ask, 'Who's that with Willie Carson?''

But having created the image of the irrepressible cheekie chappie, he failed to exploit it. Rather than employ someone to take him into the lucrative advertising business, he maintained the more personal hands-on approach, which in the short term saved him money but severely limited his potential.

Others, however, testify to Carson's generosity. Jimmy Lindley, once a former weighing room rival and now television commentator and racing journalist, says: 'I have never known him not to hold up his corner. When I ran the international jockeys' series against South Africa he would ride for the price of the air ticket. He would get off the plane jet-lagged but still go out and ride just to keep the event going. He was a marvellous ambassador.'

Ian Tedford, the former director of the Jockey Training School in Hong Kong, remembers Carson's visits to the colony. 'When the top riders were in the Far East I would ask them to come and advise the boys on how to become jockeys. Willie and Joe Mercer were two of the few who would come without being paid. Willie was brilliant. He would even join the boys' PT, climbing up and down ropes with them. They were all very small and Willie would stress that they should never be afraid, pointing out that he too was tiny. One morning, to prove his point, he took a horse into the dressage ring, which was not that big. He had it going flat out and then pulled it up within forty metres. He convinced them that being small was not the handicap they feared it would be; the knack, he told them, was all in the timing. I have nothing but admiration for Willie Carson. He readily gave his time to help the youngsters and that was a fine gesture.'

Carson will admit the attraction of money, but denies it is his sole motivation. 'Money drives me, of course it does,' he says, 'but it is more than just money. There is achievement and the fact I enjoy racing. I like winning. Sometimes when I drive to a small meeting I ask myself why I bother. But it is the only way, the way I was brought up. To strive and strive and strive.'

Carson's striving has paid off handsomely. As 1990 ended he could reflect on another strand of his outlook on life. 'Riding good horses is what keeps me going,' is an ever-present theme. With the formidable equine army of Sheikh Hamdan at his disposal and an apparently limitless fund of drive and enthusiasm, he could look to the future in the certainty that it held plenty more good horses.

CHAPTER EIGHTEEN

1991

Like Lester Piggott, Willie Carson seems to go on for ever. Twice in the 1991 season the seemingly ageless veterans were the principals in the finishes of important races. In the Greenham Stakes at Newbury in April, as Carson launched a desperate attack on the favourite, Mukaddamah, the sight of the now 55-year-old maestro peering enigmatically over his shoulder at his toiling rival must have seemed like the revival of a lifelong nightmare. Particularly as a few days earlier in the *Daily Mirror*, Carson had surprisingly been quoted as taunting Piggott for having been so ill-advised as to have made a come-back.

Then, in the 1,000 Guineas eleven days later, Carson took a sweet revenge when Sheikh Hamdan's brilliant filly, Shadayid, comfortably outpaced the Lester Piggott-ridden Kooyonga. The scribes gravely recorded the next morning that both Carson and Piggott were grandfathers and that their combined ages totalled 103 years.

It is a well-tried maxim in racing that, provided their nerves hold good, top-class jockeys, like vintage wine, improve with age. 'You seem to get more time to think,' Piggott once said. 'The more experience you get, the quicker you see trouble building up ahead and the easier it is to take avoiding action.' Carson's naturally light body-weight has always given him an advantage over his more heavily built rivals. That factor, combined with a superb ability to organise his life to ensure maximum time for rest and recuperation, is now paying dividends as he continues to power his way relentlessly forward less than a year away from his fiftieth birthday.

1991 started with Carson even more firmly established as contract rider to the previous season's leading owner, Sheikh Hamdan Al Maktoum. John Dunlop, Salsabil's trainer, appeared to hold the aces as far as the Classics were concerned. Shadayid, who had given the jockey, trainer and owner their third victory in the previous four seasons in the Prix Marcel Boussac on Prix de l'Arc de Triomphe Day, was already a short-priced favourite to give the trio their second consecutive win in the 1,000 Guineas.

On the 2,000 Guineas front, Dunlop's highly regarded Marju, an impressive winner of a minor race as a two-year-old at York on his only appearance, was thought likely to be Carson's mount in the first of the colt's Classics. Interestingly, Carson hardly ever visits Arundel. Dunlop, operating in the beautiful surroundings of Arundel Park, likes to increase the severity of a Classic horse's work-load progressively, by upgrading the standards of galloping companions. For this process he has his own highly experienced riders and therefore sees no need for jockeys to be present.

A visit to Arundel in early April found the trainer delighted with Shadayid's home work but perplexed about that of Marju, who had adopted the bewildering habit of slowing down once he had moved alongside the horse leading him in his gallops. However, the trainer's doubts were laid at rest when Marju passed his preliminary test with flying colours in the Craven Stakes at Newmarket. Marju quickened impressively in the last furlong to win by one and half lengths and become favourite for the Guineas.

Willie after winning the 1,000 Guineas on Shadayid in 1991, with the owner, Hamdan Al Maktoum — the man who has put Carson right back at the top of his profession

At Newbury on the Friday Shadayid was almost as impressive as had been Salsabil the previous year when sprinting home by three lengths in the Fred Darling Stakes. And by the end of the afternoon Sheikh Hamdan's filly was odds on for the Guineas.

Carson was in a triumphant mood at Newmarket on 1,000 Guineas day the following week, after Shadayid had given the Scotsman his sixteenth British Classic win, in the process thwarting Piggott's attempt to land his thirtieth on Kooyonga. 'I may

Willie tosses his trophy in triumph
after the 1991 1,000 Guineas victory

not be getting any younger but the horses are certainly getting better,' Carson said, as the bookmakers made Shadayid favourite to land the Guineas-Oaks double. Throughout her career Shadayid's highly strung temperament had given Dunlop cause for concern. But it was noticeable at Newmarket that despite her restless jogging, the grey filly had her nerves well under control and Carson was therefore able to husband her resources for a late burst of speed. But with stamina doubts on both sides of her pedigree, Shadayid's ability to last the mile and a half at Epsom was by no means certain.

On the Saturday hopes of both the stable and Carson of completing the Guineas double were naturally high. But disaster struck when Marju, veered to the right leaving the stalls, was never racing on an even keel before finishing a disappointing eleventh behind Mystiko. At the time both the jockey and the trainer were mystified, but next morning the beaten 6–4 favourite was found to be lame.

The Guineas over, the usual hunt for the likely winners of the Derby and the Oaks became the main preoccupation. The puzzle was even more perplexing than usual. Marju's dam had already produced one Derby winner in Salsabil. And Dunlop, rightly as it turned out, believed that the three-year-old's sire, Last Tycoon, possessed enough elements of stamina in his pedigree to prove capable of siring a top-class middle-distance performer.

However, although Carson's choice of Oaks mount was soon settled as Sheikh Hamdan decided in favour of running Shadayid, the jockey went on searching for Derby alternatives as Marju's recovery was by no means certain. One by one the possibles disappointed and the issue was only settled when Dunlop won the race against time and Marju was passed fit to take his chance the weekend before Epsom.

Virtually friendless in the market at 14–1, Carson and Marju acquitted themselves and Dunlop with tremendous credit. As the twenty-four-year-old Alan Munro sent Generous smoothly into the lead early in the straight, Carson was launching an attack up the far rails on Marju. Battling away with courageous zest in the final two furlongs, Marju finished second, five lengths behind Generous and seven lengths ahead of the Irish-trained Star of Gdansk. As usually happens in the blue riband of the turf, stamina had won the day.

Unfortunately those who ignored the tenets of breeding for middle-distance Classics and made Shadayid even-money favourite for the Oaks suffered the same fate as those who had trusted Mystiko and Hector Protector in the Derby. As with Marju three days earlier, Dunlop had the grey filly trained to the minute with temperament well under control. Whatever Carson's original battle plan had been, resourceful and intelligent riding by Christy Roche on Jet Ski Lady was the principal reason for Shadayid's downfall. Roche, the man who had also ridden Secreto to that shock defeat of El Gran Senor in the 1984 Derby, made virtually every yard of the running on Jet Ski Lady. Carson, enjoying a trouble-free run on the inside down the hill and round Tattenham Corner, reached a challenging position early in the straight. But Roche had been gradually stepping up the gallop for some time and it was clear two furlongs from home that the favourite's strength had been sapped. As Jet Ski Lady drew further and further ahead to win by ten lengths, Shadayid continued to weaken and finally lost second place by three-quarters of a length to Shamshir. 'As you could all see for yourselves, she just didn't stay,' said Carson sadly, his confident pre-race assertions for once having been proved to be wide of the mark.

Despite his lack of success in the mid-season Classics Carson was continuing to ride like a man inspired, his strength and vigour unimpaired and his tactical sense and judgement of pace as sound as ever. Amazingly, the weekend before Royal Ascot he was the season's leading rider, two winners ahead of Pat Eddery, the reigning champion and ten years Carson's junior.

So where does Carson stand among the outstanding riders of the past forty years?

His ranking of third behind Sir Gordon Richards and Lester Piggott in the number of races won during their careers, would certainly not be very wide of the mark.

One of my most treasured racing memories came on a wintry afternoon at Newmarket over ten years ago. The occasion was a humble maiden event; the protagonists in a memorable finish, Piggott and Carson, whose mount had looked a certain winner until an almost superhuman whirlwind effort by the maestro had put the issue in doubt close to home. A cameo of Carson sitting motionless on his mount as the announcer started to give the result of the photo-finish remains sharply imprinted on the mind. An expression of disgust on the rider's face as he threw the reins angrily over the horse's head demonstrated louder than any words that his arch rival had prevailed. 'What can I do to beat him?' was the implicit caption.

In reality there has never been much between the two men and of all the riders I have watched during my time as a racing journalist, Carson, Piggott and Eddery are the three men, in no particular order of merit, whom I have liked to have on my side when the chips are down. Steve Cauthen, of course, is at least as effective as this trio tactically, but perhaps not quite as strong in a finish. It has been suggested that Carson lacked the finesse and therefore the full effectiveness of Piggott and Scobie Breasley. Alan Amies, senior *Raceform* racereader, sharply disagrees. 'I prefer Willie to both Scobie and Lester. You can see what he's doing all the time which is so exciting to watch. Of course Pat Eddery and Steve Cauthen are marvellous jockeys too. But Eddery makes some bad errors and I don't think Steve's as hungry as he was.' Amies sums up: 'Tactically he gives ground to no man, and despite his light weight he's at least the equal of the other top men in strength. He's terrific. There's no one I'd rather have on my side, particularly when my own money's on.'

Having known Carson reasonably well on a professional basis for a number of years, the feature of his make-up that keeps striking home is his intelligence. Apart from his phenomenal energy, the secret of his continuing success probably lies in the way he has applied that intelligence to the organisation of his daily life and to his riding. Above all, William Hunter Carson has been a tremendously powerful influence for good in the sport from which he derives his not inconsiderable livelihood. His uncompromising honesty, coupled with an inflexible determination to give of his best, stand out like a beacon. These qualities, coupled with his cheerful and wisecracking public image, have earned him universal respect and admiration.

In attempting to give an objective picture of his larger-than-life personality, Carson's thriftiness and ruthlessness cannot be overlooked. The jockey is as tough and unyielding as the rock of his native Stirling. But his remarkable rags-to-riches story would never have taken place without his indomitable resolution and powers of self-motivation.

Three women have been powerful influences in Carson's life: his mother, his first wife Carole, and now Elaine. As capable and ambitious as her husband, the Cheshire farmer's daughter works all the hours God sends to ensure her husband's comfort and to further his career. The jockey's parents, Tommy and May, divide their time between Newmarket and Gloucestershire. 'They're both in their seventies,' says Mike Cattermole, 'May's very much the livewire, as bright as a button. Willie gets his perky attitude from her. Tommy's more of a serious fellow. He's been plagued by ill-health for some years now. That's probably where Willie gets the other side of his nature from.'

Willie's strength and determination in a finish is undimmed
by the passing years . . . At Royal Ascot in June 1991,
Carson wins a thrilling race for the St James' Palace Stakes
on Marju by a head from Second Set.

*Willie Carson winning the Newgate Stud
Middle Park Stakes at Newmarket on the
Robert Sangster-owned Rodrigo de Triano,
October 1991*

CHAPTER NINETEEN

1992

Carson ended 1991 with 155 winners, ten behind the champion Pat Eddery. Close though he finished, Carson had never quite been able to exert sufficient pressure to offer a realistic hope of a sixth jockeys' championship.

He did, however, claim two other distinctions. He collected the highest win and prize-money total of any rider that season, almost £2.3 million, and, remarkably for a man in the shadow of his fiftieth birthday, he had the most rides: 890.

The year was also notable for his burgeoning association with the first-season trainer Peter Chapple-Hyam, who had been installed at Manton, the multi-million pound complex in Wiltshire, by Robert Sangster. Chapple-Hyam had the start all young trainers dream about. Not only did he have one good horse, he had two: Rodrigo de Triano and Dr Devious.

Carson enjoyed a spectacular autumn on both. Rodrigo de Triano took his score to five wins from five starts with victories in the Champagne Stakes at Doncaster and the Middle Park Stakes at Newmarket, two of the season's most demanding two-year-old tests. Dr Devious landed another searching examination of the juveniles, the Dewhurst Stakes at Newmarket.

As autumn slipped into winter, Carson had plenty to ponder. Rodrigo de Triano, named after the lookout on Columbus's voyage who first sighted the Americas, was officially rated the best British-trained two-year-old of 1991, second in Europe only to Arazi. The bookmakers had already made him favourite for the 2,000 Guineas.

Dr Devious was also making a long-range impression on a Classic market. He too was a favourite, in his case for the Derby. Here indeed was top-class material with which Carson could work.

His retaining owner, Hamdan Al Maktoum, had enjoyed a less successful time with his two-year-olds but the instinct and judgement which had served Carson well throughout his career were as keen as ever.

Although Muhtarram, trained at Newmarket by John Gosden, had only two minor successes to his name, Carson was convinced that if Sheikh Hamdan was to have a horse of Classic standard in 1992 this would be the one. His belief in Muhtarram was absolutely right, but perversely the colt would also be his nemesis, at least in the early part of the season.

Carson was back on board Rodrigo de Triano for the colt's seasonal debut, the Greenham Stakes at Newbury. Chapple-Hyam felt Rodrigo would benefit from the run, and there was also a question mark about his ability to handle ground which was becoming increasingly tacky.

The trainer's reservations were justified. Carson produced Rodrigo de Triano to challenge a furlong out but the tank was quickly empty. He came home fourth to the French-trained Lion Cavern, beaten about three lengths.

Although Rodrigo de Triano's reputation had taken a pummelling, Chapple-Hyam was already preparing to fight another day. 'It was my fault,' he declared. 'I was too easy on him. By the time Newmarket and the 2,000 Guineas comes along he'll be like a caged tiger.'

Five days after Rodrigo de Triano's seasonal debut Muhtarram reappeared in the Craven Stakes at Newmarket. He turned in an encouraging performance, holding his own in company significantly stronger than he had tackled previously until lack of race fitness told in the final furlong. At the line he was six lengths fourth to the Michael Stoute-trained Alnasr Alwasheek.

Despite the defeat of his Classic hopefuls, Carson still had plenty to play for. There is a world of difference between Classic trials and the Classics themselves; horses often improve for their first race of the season and both trainers believed their charges had more to offer. So far, so good.

But then came the decision which would shape Carson's year. Muhtarram had been considered more likely to shine over middle distances than the mile of the 2,000 Guineas, leaving Carson no problems in pursuing his association with Rodrigo de Triano.

However, as Guineas day approached it was announced that Muhtarram would run and Carson, bound by his retainer, would ride. Chapple-Hyam was left without a jockey, but good horses soon attract good jockeys. Enter Lester Piggott.

With Piggott stepping in for Carson, Rodrigo de Triano was sent off at 6–1 third favourite for the 2,000 Guineas. Alnasr Alwasheek, translated from the Arabic as 'imminent victory', carried plenty of market confidence at 5–2 favourite with Carson's mount Muhtarram all but unconsidered at 25–1.

Like a drowning man, Carson must have seen his past flash before his eyes. As he struggled to find room to challenge on Muhtarram, Piggott swept majestically past on Rodrigo de Triano to land the thirtieth British Classic of his career. As Rodrigo de Triano settled the issue with the telling acceleration that would become his hallmark, Carson had to be content with fifth, although beaten little more than two lengths.

Piggott, for so long the spectre that haunted Carson's struggle to establish himself, was back as potent as ever. The irony was razor sharp. When Piggott announced his intention to return to race riding some eighteen months earlier, Carson's voice

*The 2,000 Guineas at Newmarket, May
1992. The one that got away – Willie
Carson on Muhtarram (second from right,
striped cap) this time has a rear view of his
old rival, Lester Piggott, winning on Rodrigo
de Triano*

*Willie at his strongest – winning the United
Breweries Fillies Stakes at Sandown on
Susurration, from Cloud Of Dust (Daryll
Holland), May 1992*

had been among the most prominent in warning Piggott that time might have taken its toll. The legend could stand revealed as just another ageing mortal.

But Piggott was not only back, he was back on a Classic winner with Carson's unwitting help. Nor was Carson's mood improved when Rodrigo de Triano went on to complete the 2,000 Guineas double by taking the Irish equivalent at the Curragh.

Mike Cattermole, Carson's agent, feared Carson would take a dim view of proceedings. 'But he took it very well,' Cattermole says. 'He had a contract with Sheikh Hamdan and as far as he was concerned that was that. He had to stand down at Newmarket but you can't ride two horses in the same race and he was tied to Muhtarram.'

Unhappily for Carson, Dr Devious also slipped through the net. He too reappeared in the Craven Stakes, in which Carson was signed up for Muhtarram, leaving Chapple-Hyam to use the American rider Cash Asmussen. Dr Devious finished a good second before leaving to run in the Kentucky Derby, in which he was unplaced. He did, however, return to Britain, and the paths of Muhtarram and Dr Devious crossed again at Epsom.

Carson was, at first, confident of Muhtarram's chance of giving him a fourth Derby. An impressive racecourse gallop had caught the eye of racing's professionals and Muhtarram was solidly supported in the betting on what was becoming the most open Derby in many years.

But heavy rain in the days before the race was against a colt known to be at his best on fast ground. Carson still felt he was in with a chance, but the softening ground was a clear disadvantage. Both his old associates, Rodrigo de Triano and Dr Devious, were in the field. Piggott, seeking his tenth Derby, had become a fixture on Rodrigo de Triano, while John Reid, an articulate and likeable Ulsterman, had been given the ride on Dr Devious.

Once more, Carson was to see a Classic won by a horse which, in different circumstances, he might have been riding. Dr Devious, always travelling well, led just over a furlong out and ran on strongly to beat St Jovite by two lengths. Muhtarram, never close enough to strike a blow, was fourth, five places ahead of Rodrigo de Triano, who was betrayed by a lack of stamina. Carson had no complaints. 'I was pleased enough with Muhtarram,' he said. 'He just wasn't fast enough.'

Muhtarram's defeat concluded what had been a relatively quiet spring. As well as missing out on the Classic-winning association with Rodrigo de Triano, and perhaps Dr Devious, his principal stables struggled to find their best form. But Carson could still demonstrate that when the horse was good enough, so was he.

Susurration's victory in a listed race at Sandown Park in May was vintage Carson. Although given instructions to make the running, Carson swiftly saw the pace was too strong. He decided instead to delay Susurration's challenge, which he delivered precisely. Produced to lead a furlong out, she had just enough in hand to repel Cloud Of Dust by a short head.

Yet for all Carson's enthusiasm he, no less than the next man, is not immune to the passage of time. He has had to make allowances. 'There is no doubt that he is easing off on the accelerator,' Cattermole says. 'I've been told not to book as many outside rides, he is very conscious of who he rides for. He doesn't want to risk falls or any possible injury, he wants to stick with the top men, the men in form.

'I've been trying to cut down, but I know that when I do he'll be asking me why I'm not booking him more rides. How close he is to retiring I don't know. Much depends on his view of whether he'll have good horses to ride next season. If not, the incentive to call it a day will be greater.

'Another factor is that "Bilko", his pilot, is past sixty and he's starting to get a bit tired. When he goes Willie might consider it too. In a way that would be the ideal, the team going out together.'

The racing scene will inevitably lose much of its colour when Carson finally decides to hang up his boots. But many avenues will obviously be open to a man with such a keen mind, such a natural love and understanding of horseflesh and such powerful connections. For his leisure time the cry of the hounds in winter will be as compelling a call as ever. Or he may decide to develop his interest further at his beloved Minster Stud. A job as racing manager to one of the Sheikhs could well become available. But as far as training is concerned he once told me, 'I wouldn't want the responsibility and hassle of becoming a public trainer. But I wouldn't mind training a few privately. Something will turn up and I'll always find plenty to do.'

As Willie enters his fiftieth year, the will to win remains undiminished by the passing years

CHRONOLOGY OF
WILLIE CARSON'S CAREER

1959: Joined Gerald Armstrong at Middleham. First ride, Marija, at Redcar on 18 May, unplaced.

1962: First winner, Pinkers Pond, at Catterick on 19 July. Only winner of the season.

1963: Transferred to Sam Armstrong at Newmarket on retirement of Gerald Armstrong. Five winners.

1964: Fifteen winners.

1965: Lost apprentice claim on Regal Bell at Redcar on 3 August. Ended season with thirty-five winners, including first big race success, Monkey Palm, in the Great St Wilfrid Handicap at Ripon.

1966: Thirty-five winners. Agreed to join Bernard van Cutsem as understudy to Lord Derby's first jockey, Doug Smith.

1967: Rode as understudy to Smith with a view to replacing him on his retirement at the end of the season. Thirty-five winners but seriously injured in car accident after the end of the season.

1968: First Derby ride, Laureate, at the age of twenty-five. Sixty-one winners in his first year as Lord Derby's jockey, despite missing the opening weeks of the season through injuries received in the car accident.

1969: Sixty-six winners; tenth in the jockeys' table.

1970: Eighty-six winners for third place in the jockeys' championship.

1971: First century of winners, 145, for second place to

Lester Piggott in the jockeys' championship.
1972: First Classic win, the 2,000 Guineas on High Top. First jockeys' title with 132 winners.
1973: Retains jockeys' title with 164 winners.
1974: Disqualified from third place in Oaks after bareback ride on Dibidale. Dibidale went on to win Irish Oaks and Yorkshire Oaks. Ended season with 129 winners.
1975: Won Champion Stakes on Rose Bowl, one of 131 wins that season. Death of Bernard van Cutsem.
1976: Joined Clive Brittain as stable jockey. Announcement that Carson would become Dick Hern's retained rider at West Ilsley from the next season. Finished year with 138 winners.
1977: Won Oaks and St Leger on the Queen's Dunfermline in her Silver Jubilee year. Also won Benson & Hedges Gold Cup at York on Relkino and steered Boldboy to five victories including the Challenge Stakes for the second time and the Vernons Sprint Cup. Rode 160 winners.
1978: Champion jockey with 182 winners from a prodigious 986 rides. Only Sir Gordon Richards had had more rides (exactly 1,000) in a season.
1979: Won Derby, Irish Derby, King George VI and Queen Elizabeth Diamond Stakes and Benson & Hedges Gold Cup on Troy. Added Irish and French St Legers on Niniski. Despite 142 winners, relinquished jockeys' title to Joe Mercer.

1980: Landed five Classics: a second successive Derby on Henbit; Oaks on Bireme; 2,000 Guineas on Known Fact; Prix du Jockey-Club (French Derby) on Policeman; and Irish Oaks on Shoot A Line. Also won Eclipse Stakes and King George VI and Queen Elizabeth Diamond Stakes on Ela-Mana-Mou. Champion jockey for the fourth time with 166 winners.

1981: Season disrupted by serious fall from Silken Knot in Yorkshire Oaks in August. Out for the remainder of the year but still finished second to champion jockey Lester Piggott with 114 winners.

1982: Won Irish Oaks on Swiftfoot but season overshadowed by mysterious defeat of Gorytus in Dewhurst Stakes at Newmarket. Rode 145 winners.

1983: Awarded OBE for services to racing in New Year Honours. Won Oaks and St Leger on Sun Princess; July Cup, William Hill Sprint Championship, Vernons Sprint Cup and Prix de l'Abbaye de Longchamp on Habibti; Ascot Gold Cup on Little Wolf. Champion jockey with 159 winners.

1984: Won King's Stand Stakes on Habibti; Yorkshire Oaks on Circus Plume. Injury while riding in Milan restricted total winners to ninety-seven.

1985: Landed King George VI and Queen Elizabeth Diamond Stakes on Petoski; Irish Oaks on Helen Street. Rode 125 winners.

1986: Victories in Ascot Gold Cup, Goodwood and Doncaster Cups on Longboat. Ended season with 130 winners.

1987: Won 2,000 Guineas and Irish 2,000 Guineas on Don't Forget Me. Rode 100 winners.

1988: Took St Leger on Minster Son, whom he bred; King's Stand Stakes on Chilibang. Better year for winners numerically, up to 130.

1989: Completed unique four-timer of 2,000 Guineas, Derby, Eclipse Stakes and King George VI and Queen Elizabeth Diamond Stakes in the same season on Nashwan. Ended with 138 winners.

1990: Won 1,000 Guineas, Oaks and Irish Derby on Salsabil; Prix de Diane on Rafha; King's Stand Stakes, Sprint Championship, Ladbroke Sprint Cup and Prix de l'Abbaye de Longchamp on Dayjur. Best season for winners, 187, but was only second in jockeys' championship to Pat Eddery.

1991: Won Craven Stakes at Newmarket on Marju, and 1,000 Guineas on Shadayid, second in the Derby on Marju on whom he won St James' Palace Stakes at Royal Ascot. Won Dewhurst Stakes on Dr Devious and Middle Park Stakes on Rodrigo de Triano, both at Newmarket. Ended season with 155 winners.

1992: Fifth in 2,000 Guineas and fourth in the Derby on Muhtarram.

ACKNOWLEDGEMENTS

The following photographers took the pictures on the pages indicated:

Gerry Cranham 2, 45, 48, 51, 52, 54, 57, 72, 89, 90, 93, 105, 113, 116, 126, 150, 151, 169, 173, 174, 177, 178, 181; *Daily Mirror* 43, 95; Tony Edenden 130, 139, 140, 144, 148, 153, 159, 161; Hulton-Deutsch 25; Trevor Jones 6, 12, 13, 83, 125, 136, 155, 156, 165, 170; Katz Pictures 158; PA-Reuters 26, 28, 29, 36, 96, 98; *Scottish Daily Record* 14, 19; George Selwyn 9, 58, 109, 115, 127, 128, 138, 147; Sport & General 20, 31, 32, 40, 41, 49, 55, 60, 62, 63, 66, 67, 68, 79, 80, 81, 85, 87, 91, 101, 103, 107, 108, 117, 118, 119; Sporting Pictures 131, 162; Whyler 16; Richard Young 100.